A Marine's Journal

Feb '67 – Feb '68

Mike Holiday

abbott press®

A DIVISION OF WRITER'S DIGEST

A Marine's Journal
Feb '67 – Feb '68

Abbott Press books may be ordered through booksellers or by contacting:

Abbott Press
1663 Liberty Drive
Bloomington, IN 47403
www.abbottpress.com
Phone: 1-866-697-5310

ISBN: 978-1-4582-0713-5 (sc)
ISBN: 978-1-4582-0712-8 (e)

Printed in the United States of America

Library of Congress Control Number: 2012922539

Abbott Press rev. date: 12/17/2012

Foreword

Not another one!

When the author, my friend, informed me he was going to write a book about the Viet Nam war experience, the first thought that popped in my head was oh no not another one! I was a youngster during this American experience, and like many readers, I too have sat through the Hollywood movies, Television documentaries, and news accounts of this era.

Although always removed from those men and women who actually served, the relentless exposure to the subject over the years had separated me even more from the significant connection I would come to know and accept while reading this book.

My friend is an enigma. The main character in his book mirrors that perfectly. Thinking back, I remember what drew me to this person early on was his wit and equally unadulterated lack of hypocrisy. He has been an entrepreneur, political analyst, teacher, mental health professional, soldier, community advocate, husband, father and above all a friend to many. I recall a story he told about a person who had significantly impacted his life.

In this story, the person tells him." You (the author) , are a bear. You put your strength on the outside, but underneath that bear is a lamb .The day you can put the lamb on the outside and the bear on the inside is the day you become a man."

Reading this journal, it became evident that the lamb is how this bear really survived his experience. Human traits are both bear and lamb but the balance is how we all survive.

My friend has taught me much about the art of balance in ones life.

The reader's journey here is all about gaining balance. How does one balance being an American while gaining acceptance and understanding of American history? How does one balance the emotions the book elicits with the bear and lamb within self? And finally, how does one balance the gray inherent in all human experience, the non-finite edges, and the bombarding choice to see the glass half empty or half full?

There are times when reading some account, some instruction, some lesson can in fact alter the way we feel about past, present and future. For me, the connection was primal.

I smelled the Water bo , I could smell the villages , I could smell the rain ,and I could smell the fear laced in each paragraph. I could see the horizon from the hills. I could see the rice paddies, I could see the children and women, I could see the strewn bodies while still animated, and I could see the duty in seeing all things as they really were.

I could hear the sniper fire, I could hear the barking orders, I could hear the wailing of trauma, and could hear the deafening silence of futility.

I could feel the curiosity, I could feel the adrenaline, I could feel the empathy, and I could feel the pain.

For me, reading the pages was living the honor, courage and duty. I go forward connected to all of it. Connected to those men and women, connected to all those who have sacrificed, connected to my country and above all connected to myself.

Thank you dear friend for the chance to stand in the balance of my being.

Bekah Lyons Phd.

Preface

This journal is based on real events that either happened to the author or someone he knew. The diary entry format was chosen as that represents the chronicled reality of the times described. Considering memories often become clouded and perceptions of particular events are varied, even when two or more people see the same event unfold, I have decided to label this as a work of fiction. While the names are fictitious, all characters in the journal are real people. The country, topography, specific military units and incidents are factual. For example, Hill 37 actually was the headquarters of 3rd Bn 7th marine regiment; at the time this journal takes place.

The purpose for writing this "journal" was not only to educate but also place the reader in the boots of the Marine in real time. For the reader to experience how it really felt for a young combat Marine in Vietnam. Viscerally come to know how he saw the war, how he internalized feelings about things he had witnessed or participated in, and ultimately how he processed being a part of war.

Despite revisionist history most of the young men who fought in this war were not dopers, potheads, murderers or baby killers as the liberal media and liberal society have painted them over the years. The Marine performs his tasks immersed in the horrors of the realities inherent in war. I hope to enlighten the reader to the concepts of honor, duty, and courage.

The written voice echoes an eighteen or nineteen year old from traditional America as his entries scribbled on paper so unfolds the coping mechanisms of a youthful patriot.

The elaboration that follows each journal entry was deliberately written using a stark no-holds-barred, factual approach. The journal entry will be written in the first person, the author being Mike Holiday. The elaboration to follow will be written in the third person, describing the details of the entry. I expect the reader to tolerate the Marine's experiences without Hollywood sanitization. How many times we hear the expression "War is hell!" but do we ever really think about war?

War is hell but sometimes necessary. Whether this war was necessary or not is still open to debate. That being said, with all that the reader will read about in this journal, I, as the author will tell you the worst thing I went through, was to come back to the United States and be treated as a monster by my fellow citizens. The movies may have depicted the scenes of shouting down men and women returning home whose sacrifice were doused in the spit of cowards. But for me it was the unspoken words the fixed glares and the thick judgment that still aches in my belly today, almost five decades later. War IS hell. War is sometimes necessary.

Honor is the byproduct of being tested and ending up looking back, knowing you did the best you could with the choices given you, when the easy road would have led to Canada. Some of us look back in wheelchairs, some with no sight, and some from the great beyond. Courage is the manifestation of honorable duty. Duty to one's country and countrymen must be worth it, or Liberty is nothing more or less than Tyranny wrapped in sheep's clothing. Like every young man or woman who fought in that war, I did my duty. I dedicate this journal to them.

5Feb: 67 What the hell am I doing here? It is pitch black dark and raining and we have landed in Vietnam, but where in Nam are we?

0410 I found out the time and had my watch adjusted to this time zone. I wonder what time it is back in the states. I am not tired. Slept most of the way across the pacific. Nice of Uncle Sam to fly us commercial jet to a war zone.

2200 Stood in line all day, for one thing or another. But the last line was weird. We were in line to see what outfit we would be assigned to. When it got to be my turn, I heard the clerk say 9th Marines, then somebody slipped him a note and he asked what my MOS was I told him radioman and he then told me I was going to the 7th Marine Regiment. 9, 7 just numbers to me.

Holiday found out weeks later that the 9th had earned the nickname the "walking dead" because they had lost so many men, especially 1st bn 9th reg. He considered himself fortunate that he did not go to the 9th, because of the desperate need for radiomen for 3rd bn 7th reg, (3/7)

> 7Feb: 67 I have never seen it rain so much and rain so hard. It rains all the time. The ground is like soup. Moving out today by chopper to a place called Chu Lai. They issued me an M-14 but no ammo.

> 0900 Got off the chopper some guy wanted to know if there was a radioman here I said yes and he took me to a tent where I was given a radio and asked to decipher some jargon.. What the hell did I know I never even went to voice radio school, but spent 10 weeks in Norfolk VA attending radio teletype and telegraph (ship to ship) learning what dots and dashes were.

He was 18, scared and came over alone, with no friends. He wasn't much on friends anyway. He didn't graduate from high school although he could have, should have, but life at home had gotten unbearable. So, like many others, he quit school and joined the Marines. He didn't know too much about the specifics of why the US was in this country, only that the US was honoring a commitment to a SEATO member, to come to their aid in the fight against communism. His name was Mike Holiday, private first class; but for the entire time he spent in country no one ever called him Mike. It was either Holiday, or Marine, or his rank.

> 8 Feb: 67 still raining, but flown out to my unit, south of Chu Lai, near twin mountains called Nui Dang and Nui Cou. They were just isolated mountains surrounded on

all sides by rice paddies. Damn this rain. Got to meet his commander Lt Morrison. Tough as nails, like all marines. Got to meet the guys too.

The Marine base camp was right at the base of Nui Dang. The ground was so drenched in water that it was like walking in soup. His stateside boots got very heavy on his feet. He was grateful when supply issued him jungle boots and jungle utilities and a poncho. He was even issued a rubber lady (air mattress) but it had a hole in it and supply would not switch it, so.....it was shit canned (thrown away) His poncho was also half of his pup tent. Either he would have to break down his tent every morning to wear his poncho and have all his gear exposed to the rain, or keep his poncho as part of his shelter and just get used to being wet all the time. His gear consisted of a dry set of jungle utes, (utilities aka uniform) socks, a towel and his shaving kit. It was important to keep his other uniform dry, so he got used to being wet. He also was issued an Ithaca made .45 caliber pistol, a remnant of WWII and he was to keep his .45 loaded at all times.

17 Feb: 67 Sgt Holden asked for 2 volunteers to replace a wounded radioman that was attached to Lima CO as an FO radioman, and the FDC radioman with the same company. Jenkins, the other "volunteer " is whining he does not want to go out in the bush, but wants to be

> FDC radioman. Ok by me. I joined the marines to fight the bad guys. Jenkins can sit in the hooch being bored.

That night, Holiday pondered what it would be like to actually go on patrol with a combat unit, instead of sitting up all night monitoring the FDC radio in the battalion com shack. He wondered if he would ever get used to walking around at night in total darkness. How would he react the first time he got shot at; would he freeze, panic, or would he do his job?

> 18 Feb: 67 Sun broke out. Went on patrol to join Lima CO. Was tired of battalion HQ anyway. All I did was take night shift as FDC radioman and during the day, put up concertina or burned shitters. I know I am only a PFC, but would rather hump through the bush than burn shitters for my tour.

This would be the only patrol Holiday would be on where he would not be wearing a 30 pound PRC 25 radio. When away from base camp, whether it be on a hill or on flat ground, marines were ordered to wear a flak jacket. These were cumbersome vests designed to protect the vital organs from explosions but were useless in protecting a man from a bullet. As time went by and the days got hotter, most marines would wear just the vest and no jersey (marines did not wear shirts, they were called jerseys). Helmets were also mandatory. Holiday hated that heavy steel pot, but at least twice on his tour he would see a helmet save a man's life; and one of those men was Holiday himself.

Holiday had no clue what actual combat would feel like. What did happen was, at the beginning of each fire fight or ambush, Holiday's heart would pump furiously and fear would grip him, but once the initial shock was over, he would feel nothing, until the firefight was over. Then he would shake. His body would tremble. His breathing would be rapid as he forced his body to calm down. But during the actual firefight, his training would take over, and he would do what he was supposed to do....in most cases.

> 27Feb: 67 Ground is drying nicely. Sgt Stoltz is my NCOIC. A fucking lifer. My FO is Charlie McCall, a black dude from Oklahoma. First black I have ever known who likes country music. He is ok, my age, 18.

McCall was a laid back, black "cowboy". Holiday, having enlisted from Newark, New Jersey and having gone to school with urban blacks, saw Charlie as a curiosity. Charlie called himself Daddy D from OKC. He was from Oklahoma City. His favorite singer was "Country Charlie Pride". Charlie was tall and thin, like Holiday himself. He had an easy laugh, was always finding humor in humorless situations and was the most affable black man, Holiday had ever met.

> 18 March: 67 Lima CO ordered to return to battalion. HQ. No reason given. Were we kicked off our last position? Wishes someone would give me a reason. The

entire company grabbed all their gear and humped it back to 3/7 base camp.

20 March: 67 Saw my first dead marine today. I saw him die, an accident.

Holiday had been assigned to help lay out concertina wire extending the battalion's perimeter by several yards. The weather had gotten very hot. He was amazed at how hot it had gotten in such a short amount of time from first entering country in the monsoon rains. He had been given a break from work detail and was just finishing his smoke when he heard a loud explosion from third platoon's area. Running up to see what was going on, several marines were already there standing around looking at a downed marine. Holiday rushed up to the scene and was stopped short in his tracks. There, before him lay a man almost blown in half. He could see the man's spine, and little else. He looked into the man's face, a young kid no older than he was himself. He saw the man look straight at him, then look away. Holiday watched the life leave his eyes. He knew the exact instant the man had died. It left him cold, numb, in shock. But Holiday found it fascinating to see life one second then nothing the next. Holiday kept staring at the dead marine, pondering what he had just witnessed, vaguely aware of being given orders to remove the body. But Holiday was frozen, could not move to obey that order.

The gunny must have realized Holiday had never actually seen death before so close up, had never seen anyone die. Rather than make an issue of it by demanding Holiday obey that order, the gunnery sgt, turned to a man he knew to be a combat veteran and ordered him to remove the body. Holiday still was standing there after the body had been taken away on a stretcher when he felt the gunny approach him and whisper in his ear. "Get used to it marine, you will see a lot of this and if you plan to survive, learn to switch off your emotions and tough it out." Without another word, the gunny was gone.

Holiday went back to his detail but said nothing the rest of the day. That night, he though a lot about life and death, wondered if there was a god and if there was, why did HE allow life to be so fragile with so much riding on how one lived one's life.

Holiday had been raised a Catholic. The Catholic Doctrine goes something like this; pleasing a loving God who sacrificed himself, so the gospel preached, to save everyone from his sins, was the ticket to salvation. If this was so, why did god make life so fragile and was not this dead man doing his duty to god and country? Had this man thought sexual thoughts and not been forgiven them before he met his tragic and sudden death? Did he have time to repent? What kind of God would set up such demanding criteria and risk anyone eternal life in such a circumstance? How loving was this god?

The dead man, Arnold was his name, was a LAW (Light Anti-tank Weapon) man. Apparently a safety pin from one of his LAWs had fallen out and as he swung the LAWs over his shoulder one had opened and blew, taking his guts and his life….just like that. Just like that!

> 28 March: 67 Went on patrol today. It turned into a firefight that lasted all damn day. Was up for bronze star, but up for court martial too. They canceled each other out. No big deal. That bronze star and a dime will get me a cup of coffee back in the world. Lost a few men today. 2 KIA's and 4 wounded. My first action. Funny thing When the shit hit the fan I wasn't scared. But when it was all over and Charlie and me were telling the cook back at battalion HQ, I started to shake. I think what I was most nervous about was how would I re-act when we got into a firefight. I guess I did ok for me to almost get the bronze star. We are still going out on patrols, even though the Army is here now. I guess we have to wait for them to set up all their gear. Hell, we marines do twice as much on half as much as these boy scouts.

The twenty-eighth of March started out mundane enough. The FO team was told they would be part of a day patrol headed by Lt. Summers. This was platoon strength. Pfc Holiday was unaware that most patrols he would be on would be no more than a squad. The platoon had started out from HQ in single file crossing acres of rice paddies. Holiday felt ok seeing how many marines were in this patrol. Charlie was ahead of him in staggered column now that a few hundred acres had been traversed. There was a vil ahead, seemed to be a larger one than average Holiday saw that there had been a bamboo fence about 8 feet high built around this village. There was a gate, opened with what was known as a highway running into and through the village. This highway was no more than a dirt road, raised from the rice paddies, wide enough for traffic to pass itself in opposite directions.

The patrol crossed the road and skirted the East side of the walled village. Holiday noticed people seemed to be hurrying towards and then past them. He didn't think much of it besides casually asking himself why people would be scurrying in this heat. Then on the right flank, he heard gunfire. It sounded like carbines, US carbines. He had been told in orientation that the VC had stockpiled carbines from WWII when they fought the Japs. Carbines made a unique sound, almost like that of a bullwhip the way it snapped in the air.

The patrol started running towards the gunfire. There was no cover, just open rice paddies with a tree line in front of them about 200 yards. The only cover was the vil, which they were leaving behind them, in pursuit of the snapping bullwhips.

The patrol made it to the tree line. The VC were nowhere to be found. Holiday had half expected to be part of a pitched battle for control of the trees. The Lt was busily conferring with S/Sgt Akers, while Charlie was busy trying to catch his breath. Charlie's eyes were as big as saucers and Holiday wondered if he looked as scared as Charlie. Holiday took a swig of water from his canteen and adjusted his PRC 25 radio on his back. It was heavy and made him sweat even more than the others, save perhaps, the A gunner for the m-60 machine gun. He carried rows and rows of belted ammo.

Finally the order was given to move out. The entire platoon jumped into the rice paddy on the far side of the tree line in an inline formation. Holiday thought this was asinine thinking one good sweep with a machine gun from the VC would cut the entire line down, even though this maneuver had been practiced in training, he never could see the purpose for it.

The next tree line was about 700 meters in front of them, but Holiday could hear small arms fired from the front and the right. They had been taught in training that when crossing open areas under fire to duck, zig and zag. Holiday would count to 5 duck and crawl first in a zig, then up for a 5 count, running and duck and zag. Holiday KNEW he was being tracked by one of the VC. He had a radio on his back and the enemy went after 3 key men in any outfit; the lieutenant, the corpsman and the radioman, not necessarily in that order. The radio was the easiest thing to spot.

Holiday could hear the ZINGS over his head as he ran. That meant the bullets were a few feet away as they passed. On occasion he could hear the CRACK, which meant they were only inches away. He knew he was being tracked. But he figured it would take a 5 count before the enemy could find him after he popped up from crawling in a different direction from where he first ducked, site him in and pull the trigger.

He could hear and sometimes see dirt or splashes from the rounds hitting the rice paddies or irrigation ditches. After about 600 meters of this popping up and down and running like hell for 5 seconds he was exhausted. He wasn't sure where Charlie was but he knew he was doing the same thing he was trying to zig when the gook thought he zagged. *"Only about 100 meters to go"*, he thought. It was at least 110 degrees. He was dehydrating, still out in the open and thinking his luck was about to run out. So Holiday decided to extend his count to 7.

Up he got and ran. 1...2...3...4...5...6...7 CRACK! He dove for the relative safety of the rice paddy, holding his helmet as he hit the deck. He felt hot metal instead of camouflage cover. He pulled off his helmet and saw that the last round had hit the seam on the top of his camouflage covering his helmet and popped it like a flower. "Charlie!" he yelled. "Charlie!" not knowing if Charlie was even close or alive to hear him. "LOOK!"

"You hit?" Charlie cried. He saw his buddy crawling towards him. "You hit?" He asked again. Holiday stuck his helmet in Charlie's face and said again "Look." "You ain't hit," Charlie screamed as he slapped the helmet away. "Don't scare me like that you mother fucker." "I ain't staying here," he went on, "We only got about 75 yards to go, as he scrambled to his feet and took off running. "Dammit, Charlie!" Holiday yelled as he got to his feet, scrambling after him.

They both ran as if their lives depended on it, which it did, and they reached the safety of the tree line. Holiday had run past his 5 count and heard one last bullet ZING past his head, but he didn't care. He was going to reach that tree line or die trying. They both hit the deck as they reached the trees gasping for breath, but both almost giddy with delight that they had done so without getting killed.

Marines were coming in from the paddies all around them. They joined up and pushed forward until they got to the other side of the trees only to find the LT and S/SGT Akers already there. Being part of the CP both Charlie and Holiday jogged low over to where they were. Charlie told the LT that they were now out too far for our mortars to do any good. Holiday felt as useful as a handle on a piss pot. All he carried was a .45 caliber automatic pistol. "Well then grab a rifle and start shooting," retorted the LT. On impulse, Holiday grabbed the rifle lying on the ground next to him and...started shooting. The enemy was in the next tree line about 200 meters in front of them. He moved down the line of broken brush and logs to get a better view. He could see the gooks firing back at them.

There was a lull in the firing. He could hear the LT yelling. "Who stole my rifle? What idiot took my goddamn rifle?" "I have it sir," Holiday responded. "You said pick up a rifle and start firing." "Not MY goddamn rifle, you moron! You can expect a court martial when we get back to the battalion!" Holiday felt a cold fear grab him, more fear than he had felt all day dodging bullets. "Holy shit!" he said to himself. LT Summers was a gung ho Marine officer, not one to half step.

S/Sgt Akers beckoned him over to him. "Listen Holiday," he whispered. "The LT was going to lead a squad to go after those gooks in front of us. In case you haven't noticed, we are taking fire from all around us. We are too far for mortar support and almost too far for artillery. We are surrounded and it is starting to get dark. I don't want to be out here when it gets dark. Your stupid act of taking the LT's rifle might have just saved a few lives. Don't worry about it. I will make it right."

Holiday felt some relief but wondered how Akers was going to get the LT to drop a court martial especially if the LT was jeopardizing men unnecessarily.

There was a lull in the fighting so they broke for chow. C Rations, tasted like crap especially cold but no one had eaten since morning chow. It had to be around 1900 now. Holiday enjoyed the quiet. There were sporadic shots from snipers, but that was all. Holiday guessed the gooks were positioning themselves to either attack or surround their platoon and then attempt an attack after it got dark.

"Saddle up" came the command from LT. Summers. His order brought all of them to the edge of the tree line facing back towards battalion HQ, the same tree line Charlie and he had dove into about 2 hours earlier. The lieutenant started sending squads across one at a time so as not to have them bunch up. As soon as the first squad was about 100 meters out into the paddies, all hell broke loose, from 3 sides. The second squad had started out with the CP. "Move out move out!" screamed LT. He grabbed Holiday by his shoulder and said, "My radioman is down, you are now my radioman, you stick close to me like stink on shit, you got that?" "Yes sir" replied Holiday.

Holiday stuck close to the lieutenant, until Summers pushed him on ahead. "Tell the rest of the platoon to wait in that next tree line until we all catch up" "Yes sir" shouted Holiday. As he began to work his way across the rice paddy with fire coming from 3 directions, a message came through over his radio. "Lima 1 actual this is Lima 6" "Lima 1" Holiday replied. "Bill what's your status?" (*Bill? Who the hell is Bill? - The captain, Lima 6, thinks he is talking to LT, Lima 1 actual. Well no time for correcting the captain*) "We are on line sweeping back towards the vil. We have men scattered all over the paddies and have taken some casualties. 2 down as far as I can tell" Holiday snapped, out of breath. "Re-group your men and I'll call to the vil to let them know you are on your way. Will you need a medevac?" "Roger on that" responded Holiday.

Holiday half drug and half carried a wounded marine to the next set of hooches. He had no idea where the lieutenant was but knew he had to get the wounded on choppers. He called over to one of the squad leaders instructing them to stand by to throw smoke, to mark their location so the medevac chopper could land to pick up the WIAs. "On whose orders?" called back the marine. "On the captain's orders" Holiday shouted back.

"The captain? How in hell …." Holiday waved his handset at the squad leader to indicate his orders came over the radio.

With no sign of the lieutenant or Sarge, Holiday heard the choppers through the din of the firefight. He immediately switched over to the medevac frequency and instructed the chopper to look for red smoke. "Negatory. Too dark for smoke," countered the pilot. "Your LZ is hot and I am not landing unless I know exactly where you are."

Holiday screamed over to the squad leader to be prepared to light up a hooch on his order, then yelled into his radio. "We are lighting a hooch right now"…

over the protestations of the pilot who was saying the VC will be lighting hooches, too, Holiday continued. "Look for the first hooch to get lit, the FIRST one, we have marines who will cover you and dammit, we have wounded that need to get out of here NOW!" "DO IT". Holiday, lowering the handset, called over to the squad leader, "Light one up NOW"

Within minutes, the choppers were on the ground, the wounded loaded and flown out. Once the helicopters were out of sight, an eerie hush fell over the entire area, like the silence found in a graveyard. Soon, Holiday could hear marines stumbling into their area, the stragglers that LT had stayed behind to gather up.

In the gloom, Sarge's huge profile seemed to loom up out of the darkness. "I want you to take the end of the column and keep the stragglers moving, Holiday. "Who got those wounded out?"

From the darkness, Akers heard "Holiday did, Sarge". "Good job marine," Akers almost whispered. "I am going to put you up for the bronze star, for taking the initiative to regroup the men and getting those wounded medevacked out of here. Now go take up the rear" "Aye aye, Sarge" Holiday muttered, and moved to the rear.

An hour later, as the platoon relaxed outside the gate leading to the village, Holiday heard the order to report to the lieutenant. As he stumbled past the line of exhausted bodies lining the road, he could hear the LT saying, "Where is that Heeero, Sarge?" "Pfc Holiday reporting as ordered," whispered Holiday. "YOU! You're the sonuvabitch that stole my rifle!"

There was a long pause before the lieutenant spoke again. "Tell you what marine, you forget about a bronze star and I'll forget about a court-martial" "OK by me sir" answered Holiday. He was relieved about not getting court-martialed. He didn't care about any medals. That bronze star and 10 cents would get him a cup of coffee, he reasoned. He didn't want to be looked at as a hero. All he wanted to do was survive his tour.

Hours later, he and Charlie were at the mess tent scarfing down a few sandwiches the cook had prepared for the platoon as they returned from the day's events. Charlie was telling the cook about the day's events, laughing, explaining how scared he had been and how scared Holiday had looked when he pointed to the camouflage cover on his helmet being blown apart. Charlie went on the give a run-down of all the events, talking excitedly and looking for humor in recounting all the events, snickering at Holiday and laughing about how the LT had threatened a court martial for "stealing" his weapon.

Embarrassed and feeling a bit ashamed at his poor judgment, Holiday interrupted "Charlie, do you realize we both could have been killed today?" This thought, just popped into his mind as Charlie recounted all the day's events. It had sent a chill down his spine and had made his stomach turn. Charlie got very quiet. *His stomach is turning too,* thought Holiday.

> 10 April: 67 Now I know why Lima Co was pulled off of their hill. The army, 5 brigades of them, comparable to 15 marine battalions literally dropped out of the sky into all of our hard fought territory and set up camp. I have never seen so many soldiers. They have HQs everywhere. Well, that's what we do, go in first and then they send the in army to mop up. All 4 companies to our battalion are now centered into battalion HQ area. Rumor is we are pulling out soon.

> 13 April: 67 Just came off patrol and literally ran into Jerry Hanks, from high school. He is with the 101st Army Airborne, cool outfit. I was going out on daily patrol and his outfit was coming in from what appeared to be an early morning patrol. Didn't have much time to say much more than hi to him.

Holiday scanned the faces of the soldiers coming back from their patrol walking in single file, when he saw a face he recognized. Here, coming towards him was the corner-back for his high school football team, Jerry Hanks. "Jerry, Jerry" He called. "Hey I see you soldier boys come in here to relieve us after all the hard work is done," Holiday snorted. "Shit no, we came in here to save your asses." They both laughed, but by then, they had passed each other: Jerry to rejoin his brigade and Holiday to patrol the area just patrolled by the 101st. They never saw each other after that one incident. Holiday was to learn, when he did finally make it back to "the world" that Jerry never did make it back...alive.

A month after discharge from the Marines, Holiday, through his father's union, had signed up for summer work in New York City. On his way to his new job, that summer before entering college, he had stopped at the town he had lived and went to high school.

He had stopped by an old girlfriend's house. When she opened the door, she had stared at him and said, "You are dead" "Well, no I am standing here in front of you," he had replied. "They told me you are dead. They said your name is on the monument put up in Monroe Park". Holiday excused himself, and hurried up to Monroe Park to see if indeed his name is on the monument honoring the local dead. His was not, but nine names of boys he had known from high school were; and Jerry's name was on that stone.

Nine all from only one town! Holiday thought how many towns, how many monuments ......how many names.

17 April: 67 Charlie got promoted to corporal. The marines are pretty chincy giving out promotions. I think it has to do with the idea that after WWII the Feds wanted to disband the USMC, so to stay in business the marines had to prove to be able to do twice as much on half as much as the army. So money is tight and promotions mean more money going out. But, hey, we do well and CAN do twice as much on half as much. I noticed Jerry Hanks was an E-4 and he went into the

army 2 months after I joined the marines. I am still an E-2. Charlie deserved making E-4. He is the warmest friendliest black I have ever met. And he knows his job.

Holiday and Charlie were hanging out in the FDC hutch when an army officer poked his head in and asked, "Where's yer ol man"? Holiday looked at him blankly. "Oh, I forgot, you jarheads call your ol man 'skipper'… where's yer skipper?" "Hell if I know" says Charlie. "Probably at Battalion HQ, soldier officer, sir."

Holiday smiled at him. Holiday turned away from the army Captain and said to Charlie," So you made corporal, congratulations, Charlie". The Captain, realizing he would get no more info from the marines in this hooch, left.

"That's CORPORAL to YOU, private, said, Sgt Stoltz, taking the captain's place at the hatchway of the hooch. Giving the sergeant a dead stare, Holiday turned to Charlie and said in as military a voice as he could muster, "Congratulations CORPORAL Charlie." Charlie just snickered into his sleeve and then said, in as dead pan a face as Holiday had given him, "Well thanks lance private first class. You know, if you work hard, practice your salute and kiss the sergeant's ass here, someday, you too can make corporal."

Charlie couldn't contain himself anymore and broke out into an uproarious laugh that made Holiday join in, but not Sgt Stoltz. He glared at Charlie and said with a sneer, "If you think this is funny, I can take those stripes away from you much easier than you got them" Looking at Holiday he continued, "If you ever hope to make lance corporal you WILL maintain your military decorum even here, got that?" "Why yes sir sergeant sir, by the way we have some lifer juice, er. I mean we have some coffee made fresh, care for some? Holiday smiled sardonically at Stoltz. The Sarge, sneering back at Holiday said, "We got new orders, pack your gear. We leave 0600 tomorrow morning; report to the radio shack, Holiday, after you have squared away your area."

> 18 April: 67 Interesting thing happened today. We were on the tarmac at Chu Lai, waiting for choppers to fly us to our new HQ. A pilot in an F–86 taxied his plane right by us and asked someone what unit we were with. Upon hearing the answer he stood up in his cockpit and saluted us. Then every plane from his squadron as it taxied by, the pilot stood up and saluted us. In 78 days on that operation, we had lost, killed or wounded, 72% of our battalion. I had been one of the Billy boot bands (newbies) replacing a dead FO radioman.

Sitting on the tarmac at Chu Lai, Holiday, was relieved that Operation De Soto was over and that the Army had come to relieve them. As was his custom, he sat alone, not caring to join the mortar men or even to hang with Charlie, who, as usual was telling jokes and recanting stories of his combat experiences to the 81 guys.

Holiday, by nature, was a quiet man. He had few friends,

growing up and had gotten used to being alone. In fact, he preferred it. In high school, Holiday was quite the intellect, but the college prep kids pretty much ignored him since, none of them lived in his neighborhood and Holiday was not allowed to "hang out" after school. The neighborhood kids never befriended him because he was such a good student and they were average at best. Holiday was considered a "greaser" by the preppies and a "preppie" by the greasers.

He didn't mind Charlie telling stories of his and Holiday's exploits in the field. When they would come off patrol, Charlie would immediately go over to the gun crews while Holiday would go to his poncho tent and sleep. Charlie was well liked. Holiday did not know if he was liked or not and didn't care.

Holiday had noticed the fighter planes as they taxied right by where his unit was waiting. He saw a pilot stand up in his cockpit and give his unit a salute. As the third pilot did so, Holiday ran up to his plane and asked why was that officer saluting grunts? The pilot shouted "Son, you gave us a lot of business"!

> 19 April: 67 In a place called Dai Loc. A French fort is here. It's on the point of the hill overlooking miles and miles of tree lines and rice paddies. If there wasn't a war on, you'd think this view beautiful. C.O. says Lima CO will be moving out to a place called Hill 52.

> 20 April: 67 On Hill 52. There is a vil on each side of the hill. Lieutenant told me they were 2 separate vils,

not one divided by the hill. Most vils in Nam follow along a foot trail strung out for yards then only a "street" or two deep. These smaller vils had all houses made of bamboo, and then maybe one or two made of stone. It reminded me of a farm area in the Deep South of 100 years ago, with one mansion and a lot of wooden huts for the slaves. Seems one of our new neighbors doesn't like us too much. Every night, from across the river, since we have been here, at the stroke of 1900 a sniper opens up and shoots 8 rounds at anything moving on top of the hill. We have dubbed him 7 o'clock Charlie.

Holiday had just spent the day trying to make friends with whatever villagers were left. All of the men and most of the teenaged boys were absent. The Marines were told if they could buy material from the villagers to help build hooches and make living on the hill more comfortable to do so. Buy, not take. The sniper had gone on a quick patrol familiarizing himself with the terrain and landmarks. It seems the reason Lima Company took this hill was to act as a force to disrupt and/or destroy that part of the Ho Chi Minh trail that went through this part of the Central Highlands.

When the grunts had first taken this hill, every night for weeks, some sniper would shoot 8 rounds at their position, hoping to hit one of the marines at 7 o'clock every night. The grunts were in the habit of shooting 2 rounds of 81's, one from each gun as an answer to the sniper. He had gotten the nickname of 7 o'clock Charlie. The grunts had made jokes about him. They would say he must be a union man, eating his dinner, then kissing his wife goodbye, would go out to "work", shoot his 8 rounds, what the union required, then head back to hearth and home. They wonder if he carried a sack lunch with him, or a thermos to keep his tea hot.

One day early on, when Lima Company had first taken the hill, Holiday, knowing it was getting close to 1900 (7 o'clock PM) had laid on the ground, right where he stood, and propping his head up with one hand, had called out to the LT, "Sir, you will need to get down soon." "Get down?" the LT had asked. "Yes sir, hit the deck, kiss the ground, repose in a prone position, hug the dirt…" Just then POW POW POW POW POW POW POW POW , 8 rounds from Charlie . Holiday watched the LT do a swan dive hitting the deck full force on his belly. "Told ya , sir" Holiday smirked. "Holiday, you are one crazy mother fucker" "Yes sir, you already told me that………sir" Holiday smiled.

This had been LT's first day on the hill. Holiday had come in with an advance unit. The entire 81 team was to be the artillery support, should the unit ever get fired upon. No one had bothered to inform the LT of 7 o'clock Charlie. But LT should have noticed marines either lying on the ground or scurrying to enter sandbagged hutches, all at the same time. But LT had been so enraptured in the sun setting and how the shadows played on the trees and how the light sparkled off the river, which ran close to the bottom of the hill, that he hadn't noticed. And............. Holiday did try to warn him.

Holiday surprised himself at how casual he had been. He knew 7 o'clock Charlie would strike. He knew the LT would be the target. Yet, he warned him in a calm manner, not feeling tense or excited or scared at all. Only 2 months in country and already he had learned to put his emotions on hold

> 21 April: 67 What a primitive country. Once away from the cities like Da Nang, or Chu Lai, you don't see any mechanical vehicles, only bicycles or people walk. The "highways" are no wider than a dirt road found in the rural west or the farm country of US. All the houses, hooches, have no more than two rooms, dirt floors with an underground shelter dug into the main room for avoiding bombs, our bombs. No electricity: candles or kerosene lanterns instead.

> We're not living much better, in hooches dug into the ground with the "roof" only 2 or three feet above ground. Charlie wants to live with a gun crew so we don't have to dig our own hooch by ourselves. Pissed me off, the lazy bum. I am making a hooch on ground level then, only 4 feet high; a 7x4x4 ft sandbag hutch. All mine. He can go fuck himself.

The Captain had somehow procured a lot of lumber to build roofs for all the hutches. Most of it was 2x6 planks. Once the sandbags were filled with dirt and the walls were built using a 3-tier system, the planks were placed across the walls, and then secured by placing 2 rows of sandbags on top of the planks. If done correctly and with a little tar these hutches became waterproof. When the marines ran out of tar, many of the men used their ponchos laid out on the roof as a sealant. Holiday, who was to go on patrols every day, or night as the case may be, kept his poncho.

The marines were kept busy building, rebuilding and modifying their hooches, and gun placements. All the while patrols kept going out, day and night, Charlie and Holiday were asked to go on most. The grunts felt with Hill 65 eleven clicks away, it would easier and better to have as fire support, access to the two 81 mortars assigned to this company. The gun crews were very good and Charlie as FO was the best. The grunts liked Charlie and tried to be as protective of him as much as they would be to a corpsman. Holiday was accepted by the grunts more readily than by the 81 gun crews. They had felt slighted when he opted to build his own hutch and not share living quarters with either of the gun crews. Sgt Stoltz, of course, had his own hooch.

The hill itself, at 52 meters above sea level, was shaped like a giant footprint with the "heel" facing towards the mountains some 3 clicks north, and the "toes" facing south, towards the river. At this time of the year, the river had receded and left a small pond about 3 acres in area, at the foot of the hill. Marines would use this pond to go wash their uniforms and bathe. It was shared by the water bo, escorted down to the pond by the young boys in the vil. They kept the Bo on the south side closest to the river while the marines used the north end closest to the hill. A hooch had been set up outside the barbed wire gate, which housed a barber and a vendor selling cokes, fresh fruits, penknives and other assorted trinkets. There were only 180 marines on that hill and already, some locals had learned to capitalize on the marine's presence.

It had taken about 3-4 weeks for the villages to get used to the marines being there. The VC had told them that if the Yankees ever came to their vil, they would be taken off in helicopters and thrown out over the sea. In fact, when Lima CO first took the hill, neither village had any men in either village save the very old. They had fled to the hills fearing death or inscription into the South Vietnamese army, ARVN for Army of the Republic of Viet Nam. When neither had happened and the marines befriended the kids, as do all GI Joes in every foreign war the US has ever fought. and bought items in lieu of taking them, the villagers had relaxed enough for the men to return and the women to act friendly. Eventually, even the young unmarried women returned.

Holiday, done with cleaning his weapon had gone down to the vil, looking for shade and a watermelon. About 4 hooches down the trail, a woman had set up a stand to sell flesh fruits. A few marines were already there. Holiday was not going out on patrol until 1900 and felt he could spend a few hours relaxing before taking a siesta during the heat of the day. He knew his 1900 patrol would not be back until 0600 the following morning.

Holiday, strolled up the bench holding all the melons, picked one then used his k-bar to cut off slices…mmmm, juicy, but warm since there was no refrigeration. He noticed a few younger children eyeing him and then looking at the melon. "They want your melon", Sgt Benson told him. "They can get their own" replied Holiday, "There's plenty here" "Those melons are for sale, not to give away to the neighborhood kids", Benson answered. Holiday began cutting off slices and handing them to the kids, who eagerly took them.

Almost immediately the woman who had sold the melon to him began berating them in Vietnamese rather loudly. Holiday looked over to Benson, confused. "What gives?" Holiday demanded, "I bought it and now I can give it to whomever I please" "It is considered very impolite to take a gift without permission from the eldest present," Benson said, pointing to a very old man, sitting across the way. "Offer him a piece, with both hands, if he accepts, then you ask him if you can then share with the children, he will approve, THEN you can give the children pieces"

Holiday, cut off a slice of the fruit walked over to the elderly man and with both hands, offered him the watermelon. The old man took a piece without looking at him. Holiday sat back down and before giving any to the children, called over to the man. The old man finally looked at him. Holiday made gestures as if to give some fruit to a child and with his eyes, asked if that would be ok. The old man finally smiled and with a nod, had given permission. Holiday cut off pieces and made sure every kid got some.

He was surprised at seeing the custom of deferring to the elder, politeness in a war torn country, which up until this moment, Holiday had seen as a backward society full of dumb, almost primitive people. And it made his heart smile to see the joy on the faces of the kids as he passed around pieces of a simple fruit.

> 7 May: 67 Almost got killed today. So what else is new? Doc was crazy with what he did. Either that or has the biggest balls of any man I have ever known. Shuster bought it today. Quiet guy. Didn't know him too well.

The platoon had taken refuge inside the confines of a shady vil. It wasn't too hot but the sun was bright and the shade offered the illusions of coolness. Holiday heard the order to move out and dutifully got in line as the platoon wound its way through the vil, towards the paddies. By the time Holiday got to the edge of the vil to jump about 3 feet into the dry rice paddies, he noticed that almost everyone had already made it across to one of two perpendicular tree lines. As he scrutinized the area ahead of him, he noticed an irrigation ditch about half way across the open terrain. He hated patrolling in the open. It made him feel naked and defenseless.

He never did see which tree line his comrades had gravitated to as he poised to jump the 3 feet into the dry paddy. Just as he jumped off he heard the sharp CRACK a carbine makes when its bullet whizzes past one's ear. The sound pushed him to his hands and knees as he heard the gurgle of a dying man immediately behind him. He scrambled towards the irrigation ditch, hoping he could make the relative cover of the upturned dirt that lined the ditch. He heard the rustle of rice plants and the panicked voice of Private Ramos praying in Spanish behind him. "Jesus Maria, don't let me die here. God, oh please don't let me die here", he heard Ramos pray.

They both heard the call for the doc, to tend to the marine shot in the throat, the marine standing right behind Holiday, just before he had jumped down into the dry paddy. Holiday KNEW that shot had been meant for him. The gooks must have seen his radio and had targeted him, the bastards. As they both lay with their faces pressed to the dirt, they heard the doc cussing that he did NOT want to walk all the way back from whence he had come. A shot rang out. Was the doc hit? "FUCK YOU. YOU BASTARDS! Holiday poked his head up to see doc walking in a tight circle, flipping off the VC! That crazy bastard was standing straight up and taking his damn time retracing his steps, all the while keeping his middle finger pointed to heaven as he continued to cuss out the VC. "Shoot me you cock suckers and let your soul rot in hell", he shouted. Doc passed within 5 feet of where Holiday and Ramos were lying in the paddy.

Ramos would not crawl any further. Both were in awe of the corpsman, strolling back to the now dead Marine. Twenty minutes passed by. A chopper came. The body was carried out to the helicopter and then doc started to walk back to wherever he had come from. Not a shot had been fired throughout this entire episode...until doc reached the safety of the tree line. Then the air erupted with a roar of small arms fire. But by then Holiday and Ramos had managed to crawl up to and sneak into the irrigation channel, running with cool and very wet water.

As the firefight raged, Holiday was trying to build up the courage to run towards wherever his patrol had gone, but he wasn't sure which tree line the LT had led them to. "Ramos, you need to switch my frequency from 81's to the grunt frequency." Holiday was too scared to try and take off his radio and perhaps give away his position to the VC. He figured Ramos could change the frequency and then he could call LT, and get a bearing. "I'm not putting my hand up that high" Ramos yelled over the din. "My goddam head is up there, you can put your fucking hand up there now do it" screamed Holiday.

Through prayers to the Virgin Mary, Ramos finally managed to hit the right frequency. While he felt his back being pushed and shoved with Ramos working at finding that frequency, Holiday sat in the ditch with his chin just above the water, watching bullet rounds kicking up the dirt on the left edge of the ditch, each round coming closer to where he was.

Holiday turned to face Ramos and yelled, "Ramos hurry up …" and saw bullets hitting the right side of the ditch. "Shit! They had us in a crossfire'…."Ramos did you get it yet"? "Yeah yeah, call, dammit, call the LT" "Lima 1 Actual this is Whiskey Lima Forward, where the hell are you?"

"Where the hell are YOU, "Holiday heard in response.

"In that irrigation ditch"

"Well get your ass out of there"

"Don't know which tree line to run to and they got us in a crossfire"

"Stand up and let me see where you are, I'll wave at you"

Holiday put his head as close to the passing water as he could.

"What's going on?" Ramos demanded. "He wants me

to stand up so he can wave at me." Holiday almost laughed.

"Jesus Maria Madre," Ramos muttered.

Holiday, braced himself, stood up and immediately sat back down as he heard shots being fired at him. He had seen the LT in the far left tree line yelling and waving his arms.

"HEY 81's! Over HERE"!

Holiday shrieked back at him, "Did you see me?"

"Affirmative, you dumbass, now get going. We will give you cover fire"

"Ramos, we need to go NOW!"

"Hell no," cried Ramos, "There is nothing out there to stop a bullet but me. At least here we have dirt to hide behind"

Holiday shouted, "Ramos, look behind me then behind you. What do you see?" Holiday watched Ramos take a look then watched his eyes get big as saucers.

"Holy shit! They got us in a crossfire"

Holiday swung is leg out over the top of the ditch, then allowed his body to follow, rolling once to clear the ditch. Then he got up and began running as if his life depended on it, which it did. He heard Ramos screaming to wait for him. The bullets were flying all around him. He kept waiting for that one bullet to hit him in the back. He hoped the radio would stop him from getting any damage. He looked up to see a line of Marines cheering him on... as if he was running for a touchdown. He felt Ramos run past him taking a grab at his jersey to help pull him along. Dammit he always was a slow runner, which is why even at 165 pounds his senior year he was a lineman and not an end or halfback.

Ramos kept going running past him after his failed attempt to grab his shirt. Holiday focused on Ramos's ass as he ran towards the cheering crowd. The closer he got the better he felt. *"Damn I may make it"*, he thought to himself. He saw the LT looming just ahead of him, legs spread, and hands on hips. Holiday slid feet first under the lieutenant's legs and yelled "SAFE" and then smiled up at LT.

"Holiday, you are one crazy mother fucker"

"Yes sir," Holiday shouted back, "But I'm alive"

The rest of the day was spent chasing after the elusive enemy. Once the Marines had broken out of the L shaped ambush, they had performed a flanking maneuver on the VC. The enemy had broken contact and fled.

Later that evening, Holiday asked the gunny why the VC had not fired on the doc when he had walked back to the wounded Marine. Gunny told him that the Buddhists believed that to kill one "touched by god" was to doom one's own soul. And they had thought Doc crazy, or "touched by god" to stand there and flip them off in plain sight of every enemy rifle. Well, so did Holiday.

> 17 May: 67 could have gotten a purple heart today, but thought, what the hell, it was only a scratch. Hope those other two guys make it ok. Those two other guys were fucked up pretty bad.

It was about 11 AM when the patrol stopped for chow. The patrol had left the hill around 0500 and most had not eaten breakfast. The Lieutenant had picked the cover and the coolness of a well-shaded abandoned vil. Holiday had the habit of heading out with an OP rather than sit around in the CP group and watching Marines kiss the brass's ass. A fire team had headed towards the edge of the vil, to keep an eye out for any VC movement in the paddies, now dry, or the tree line beyond. Holiday jogged to try and catch up with the fire team. This part of the vil was on high ground, at least 8 feet higher than the paddies and the irrigation ditch that was carved through the length of the vil. To get from one high point to the other one had to shuffle down the one side and go through a hedgerow, almost 15 feet high on the other side of the ditch. The hedge had a small space to walk through.

As the one young Marine tried to push his way to the

other side of the hedge, Holiday felt a great force throw him into the air, in concert with a loud explosion. Holiday landed smack on his buttocks, and dazed, looked down into the ditch to see the carnage.

The VC had buried two chicom (CHInese COMmunist) grenades, one on each side of the break in the hedge row and tied the pins together with a trip wire. Anyone walking through would trip the wire which would pull out both pins from the grenades.

The lead marine had blood gushing out of his chest, while the marine behind him was holding his crotch and lower abdomen. Holiday was screaming for the doc. He saw a dozen Marines running behind him to his position. Doc saw him first and asked out of breath where was he hit. Holiday could do no more than yell, "Not me doc, them" as he pointed repeatedly to the two wounded comrades writhing in pain, lying in the ditch.

As Doc scurried down the slope, Holiday began calling for a medevac, even before the LT ordered him to. Those two men were hurt bad. Within minutes, Holiday heard a chopper landing in the paddies just to his right. Ch-34, Holiday thought from the sound of the engine and props. Holiday learned later that a colonel had been flying in the area on a recon mission and had ordered his chopper down to use as a medevac chopper.

Apparently there were no available medevac choppers, since all were tied up on some Army firefight.

Holiday began noticing throbbing pain from both of his shins. Looking down he only then realized the shrapnel that had hit the side of the slope had climbed up high enough to lodge hot pieces into both of his legs. He spent the next few minutes gritting his teeth as he pulled out the hot shrapnel from his legs. He was surprised to see that he was not bleeding much, only from the largest wound.

As he heard the chopper fly out of earshot, with both wounded Marines, he saw the doc sit next to him and light up a smoke. He noticed his hands were shaking. "How did I do, the doc almost whispered" but before he could reply, the doc continued, "This is the first time I really had to try and save a man's life."

"Not bad doc," Holiday replied, " 'cept you forgot something…me".

"Oh shit," gasped doc, "Where you hit?"

"The shins, doc, "responded Holiday, "but it doesn't hurt too bad, burns more than anything."

Doc opened up some battle dressing, then cleaned out the wounds as best he could while Holiday grunted in pain. Doc dressed and wrapped the wounds, then asked if Holiday could stand and walk.

"Sure doc" groaned Holiday.

"The heat from the shrapnel cauterized your wounds," said doc, "You should be OK".

Holiday walked the rest of the day's patrol with his shins bandaged, at times hobbling in pain, but he never complained. Doc had forgotten to list him for the Purple Heart and Holiday never reminded him. He felt the other two Marines deserved theirs while he didn't.

> 2 June: 67 Bad firefight today. Some of those in the rear with the gear gang are so stupid. I bet when they got out of the Corps, they will become bureaucrats. Whatever they see on paper is their reality, never mind what the truth is.

Holiday found himself flat on his face, bullets whizzing right over his head. *"Damn"* thought Holiday, *"The Gooks usually wait until we are out in the open before ambushing us. But we are in this vil with a few stone buildings and plenty of trees to hide behind. Must be more of them than usual for them to start this while we are still in the vil"*

Holiday was lying on his belly facing north. There was a huge stone building to his immediate right. He could see chips of stone flying off the wall from where the bullets were hitting. The enemy was to the west and north of his position. The LT was lying about 4 feet away, screaming at him to get a fire mission going. Holiday didn't need to be told twice.

"Crepe Myrtle Whisky, this is Whiskey Lima Forward, Fire mission".

This patrol had followed the river down from their hill and they were closer to battalion than they were their own hill. Hill 65 was closer as well, but Holiday knew that the gunners on Hill 37 were better than those on Hill 65. They were actually in the TAOR (tactical area of operations region) of both hills.

Charlie was nowhere to be found, so Holiday had to call this in by himself. LT was barking coordinates at him, yelling for HE (high explosive) and not a white phosphorous marker round. He must be pretty certain he knew where the Gooks were, or was trying to knock out the heavy machine gun fire ASAP that had the entire platoon hugging the dirt.

"What the fuck do you mean you won't clear this fire mission", Holiday was screaming into his phone.

"Be advised foul language will not be tolerated when calling in fire missions," the FDC radioman answered.

Holiday stared incredulously at his handset.

"Where are those HE rounds Holiday?" asked LT.

"I am getting a lecture on proper radio protocol. I said 'fuck' and he is making an issue of it" responded

Holiday. "And he said there are friendlies in the area but won't identify who the friendlies are supposed to be".

"Gimme that damn hand set," shouted LT as Holiday began crawling towards him.

The Lieutenant grabbed the phone and Holiday heard him screaming, "This is Lima one ACTUAL, we ARE the fucking friendlies, you fucking moron. I want 10 fucking rounds of fucking HE, Fucking NOW! And I suggest you do not lecture me on proper radio procedure, you fucking moron!" "Here" LT yelled as he threw the handset back at Holiday, "I don't think you will be getting anymore lessons on manners, now call in those coordinates again".

Within seconds 10 rounds of 81 mortars were falling on the tree line to the west. "Call in 10 at these coordinates, "LT shouted, giving Holiday new numbers for the tree line to their north. Holiday did what he was told. After the last explosion echoed off there was an eerie silence surrounding the platoon. After the deafening noise of the past 30 minutes, it struck Holiday as unnatural.

LT started barking orders re-positioning marines. Holiday went off to find Charlie to see if he was OK. Holiday found him on the back side of the stone building leaning up against the wall.

"How the hell did you wind up here? ", inquired Holiday.

"The bullets were coming from that-a-way," Charlie pointed over his shoulder, "So I came this-a-way"

Charlie laughed. Holiday shook his head, then sat down next to him. *Nervous laughter,* Holiday thought to himself.

"So," Charlie started, "Did you call in that fire mission by yourself?"

"LT called in the coordinates, Charlie and we couldn't find you, so I guess you are fired for dereliction of duty..."

Charlie bust out laughing, "Fire me. Fire me" he chortled, "Get me OUT of this fucking country".

Holiday joined in the chuckle. Both leaned back against the wall. Holiday sighed.

The quiet was a comfort after having one's emotions heightened by the chaos of a few minutes ago. Holiday usually did not feel the fear until after a firefight, but this time, they had been caught flat-footed and the VC had put out so much firepower in the initial burst of action, that Holiday felt the almost overwhelming fear grab him in the chest. It didn't help to see machine gun fire rake the wall where he had been standing, right after he had dived for cover.

Someday, he thought to himself, *I will not be so quick to move, or I will be in the wrong place at the wrong time and get hit. I hope it is in the head so I don't suffer before I die.* At that instant a shot rang out. The bullet passed so close to his head that he felt the chips from the wall shoot back at his face, one piece grazing his cheek just below the right eye. Both he and Charlie dove straight forward, their hearts pumping furiously. They looked at each other. Holiday thought his eyes must be as big as Charlie's looking back at him.

"Back to work, Charlie. And you are re-hired." They both started crawling towards the corner of the building looking for LT.

The firefight had begun again in earnest.

> 21 June: 67 Was on Hill 10 last night, on our way back to our hill when it got overrun. When our battalion moved north from south of Chu Lai we had our companies spread out over a large area. Hill 52 was Lima Company. Mike Company had Hill 37, our battalion HQ. India Company had Hill 10 and Hill 41 and Kilo Company had Hill 65. It seems the FO and his radioman for India Co had been lost, so Battalion made us TAD. Hope our guys in Lima can live without us for a few days. Charlie has a buddy in this company I think maybe he volunteered us. No big deal, it's just that his timing sucked.

Holiday and Charlie were tired from humping most of the morning. *We get TAD and the bastards can't even get us a ride to the gate. We had to walk in from the main highway. We are just snuffies I guess,* thought Holiday.

"Yo Holiday" Charlie called, "Let's get off this road and

cut through the field here . We can knock off a good 3-400 yards this way"

"Sure, Charlie" mumbled Holiday, whatever.

A few minutes later, and they were dodging barbed wire, and stakes of barbed tangle foot.

"Hey! Hey!" Holiday looked up to see Charlie waving at a few marines who seemed to be waving back at them from the hilltop of their base camp. Hill 10; not all that high, just a bump in large field.

"There's my buddy," Charlie called over to Holiday. Holiday could hear his buddy yelling out, "You dumb fuck" *Some buddy*

"You are surrounded by booby traps. Why didn't you take the road up?"

Uh Oh Charlie in his eagerness in wanting to cut off some walking, had stumbled into an area, where marines has set up trip wires, grenades and other booby traps.

They gingerly made their way up past all the booby traps, listening to instructions from the marines on the hill, as they called down to them where to step. Once safe and on top of the hill, Holiday thought to himself, too easy, getting up here. If they really want to deter the enemy they will have to do better than that.

After reporting in the company commander, Charlie went off to spend time with his buddy. Holiday, with nothing else to do, inspected the perimeter, where the machine guns had been set up for cross fires, how the booby traps were set up, some which could not be seen and some which were in plain sight. After a while he wandered over to the 81 gun crews. He was asking some of the men if night defensive fire missions had been pre plotted, as he and Charlie had done on their hill 52. He was surprised at the hostility he encountered.

Did he think he was the CO? Was he bucking for officer? Who in hell did he think he was telling these guys how to do their job on their hill? In Holiday's mind, it was common sense to set up pre plotted fire missions, just in case one got attacked. He thought they would be grateful for his input since it might save their lives one day. With one last snide remark ringing in his ear, Holiday drifted away from the gun pits, FDC bunker and any one identified as an 81 mortar man.

That evening after chow, he hung out in the CP bunker, playing a game of poker in lieu of staying with an 81 gun crew, when, about midnight, the shit hit the fan. He could hear sporadic gunfire at first. A marine sentry came running into the bunker, "Sir" he addressed the Captain, "I think the gooks are going to try to run us over"

"No need to exaggerate, there marine", said the Captain

stoically as he slowly put on his flak jacket and helmet. The sporadic gunfire had turned into sustained bursts, then it seemed as if gunfire had erupted all over the hill from every direction. Holiday could hear shouting, grenades going off, and incoming bullets hitting the sandbagged bunker he was standing in.

The Captain shouted as he headed towards the hatchway, "Find my radioman", to no one in particular, then turning towards Holiday said tersely, "You are the radioman, until you are relieved. You call battalion and inform them we are being attacked." "SIR" Holiday replied.

Holiday did as he was ordered. Then turning up the speaker on the radio, he ventured towards the outer hatch trying to get a glimpse of what was going on outside. A sudden chill went down his spine. *If they overrun us, they will go after the CP and blow it up.* Drawing his Ithaca made .45 pistol, Holiday pushed through the poncho being used as a door to block out the light from shining outside. Four feet in front of the hatch was a retainer wall that had been built out of sandbags, running parallel to the wall of the hooch. The ground sloped slightly up from the hatch so the wall had less and less rows of sandbags, the further along it went. Holiday got to a point where he could look over the wall. What he saw seemed to come right out of a Hollywood movie.

There was chaos everywhere he looked. He could see VC running and shooting spurts of fire from burp guns or AK's, Marines shooting back, explosions going off. Over towards the 81 gun pit he could see one of the marines who had scorned him earlier in the day, waving the tube of his 81 gun back and forth in front of him like a baseball bat. It seems the VC wanted that gun. Suddenly Holiday saw the man slump in a heap. An instant later, a VC took the tube from his dead hands and ran off into the night.

The action was happening very fast, everywhere he looked. He wanted to stay close enough to the radio to hear it but also wanted to be outside to defend the radio and himself should the gooks figure out where the CP bunker was. Out of the darkness, coming straight towards him, Holiday saw a VC holding a bayoneted rifle that was aimed right at his belly.

Holiday felt his guts begin to turn as he spun to face the enemy and pointing his .45 at the man, let loose 7 rounds. The man and the bayonet kept coming. Dropping out the expired clip and backing up as he smacked the second clip into the pistol, Holiday drew back the slide and began firing almost point blank at the bayonet and the body behind it.

Holiday could feel himself literally backed up against the wall as he fired one round after another at the steel blade aimed at his gut, With his last round fired, the enemy fell, not 2 paces from his feet. Holiday could feel his heart pumping and his breath coming in gasps, as he wiped the sweat from his forehead that hadn't been there an instant ago.

Almost in panic, Holiday ran his last clip into the pistol and resolving to use his ammo sparingly started looking for close targets to shoot at. He marveled at how 7 -14 rounds fired at that VC had not stopped him in his tracks as he had always been told would happen when hit by a .45 round.

Suddenly he heard the radio barking. Hastening inside the hutch, Holiday grabbed the handset, and gave an assessment of what he thought the status of the hill was. The captain came in hurriedly, and grabbing the handset from his grasp, informed battalion that although the hill had been over run, and he had sustained heavy casualties, he had managed to drive the enemy from the hill and things were now under control. It struck Holiday as odd that the Captain used the pronoun "I" in lieu of "we" to describe who had secured the hill.

Holiday left the hooch and walked out into the chaos and smell of death that hung heavy in the air. Charlie struggled up to him, leaning over to whisper in his ear, so no one could hear; Charlie said to Holiday, "If these bastards had had night defense pre plots, some of this might have been avoided. Holiday swallowed hard and looking at Charlie full face, he saw tears, even in the darkness, run down Charlie's cheeks

"God damn them god damn them" Charlie mumbled. Holiday mumbled back "I think he did Charlie"

The following morning, the marines were wandering all over the hill assessing the damage done. Gun pits had been blown to smithereens, broken sand bags were all over the place and dead bodies of VC lay on the ground, on top of hooches and on the sides of the hill. Holiday went with a few others to check out the dead for booby traps. The VC had a habit of booby trapping their dead in hopes of killing more Americans. Holiday came across a body, face down, hands, gripped in death on the wires of a Claymore mine. Claymores were electrically triggered mines designed to cut a swath of destruction, like grapeshot used to do on frigates and sailing war ships a century previous.

He saw no wounds on the dead man and wondered how he died. No shrapnel wounds that he could see, no bullet holes. Holiday gingerly turned the body over, careful of booby traps; rigor mortise had already begun to set in. He stared at the body; the face had gone flat from lying in the dirt. Finally Holiday noticed a small hole in the brow of the dead man. This VC had crawled up to the Claymore with the idea of turning it around to fire back at his enemy, the Marines, but apparently in his attempt a Marine had triggered the mine and one bb from the mine had pierced his brain, entering through his eyebrow, enough to kill him dead. Amazing how fragile life is.

> 22 June: 67 In 3 days I will be 19. Charlie and I just got back from a TAD on Hill 10. They, we, had gotten overrun, lost a few good men. Now we are on Hill 41 headed back to our own hill and Charlie tells me the Funewgy LT wants to use us for patrols tonight. Shit. Hell, it might be safer out there than on the hill if the gooks take a notion to hit this hill, except I don't trust the new LT. It's going to be a hot night

"Marine"! Holiday looked over his shoulder to see the funewgy LT headed towards him. "Sir"?

"You and your FO are going out on ambushes with me tonight; travel light, one canteen, no chow, nothing that rattles"

"Sir, a second canteen will not make any more noise, and will not add to the weight, and it will come in handy.........." "I heard about you Holiday", the lieutenant interrupted, "If you come out with two canteens, I will bust your ass. *Whadaya gonna do, send me to Nam?*

"Yes, SIR!" "Do NOT bring TWO; I say again TWO canteens, Yes sir"! Against all his training that said not to salute an officer in the bush, Holiday brought himself to rigid attention and saluted......smartly. *Damn! No sniper saw that.* Holiday did an about face and promptly went to find his radio and other gear.

Holiday saw Charlie coming towards him shaking his head.

"This is crazy" Charlie was saying. "That rookie LT wants to set up a series of ambushes tonight and I ain't up to it, not after last night."

"Say you are sick, Charlie." Do you trust me to call in fire missions without you?", inquired Holiday.

"Hell yeah I am sick. My guts can't stop turning from last night, and yeah I think you can handle it" replied his friend.

Holiday watched a grin slowly come across Charlie's face. Reaching out to put a hand on his shoulder, Charlie said, "For a white guy, you are alright" "I think I am coming down with a tummy ache; maybe I'm pregnant". Then laughing out loud, Charlie walked away, shaking his head, humming "Kiss an angel good morning", a Charlie Pride tune . Holiday had always thought that was odd that a black guy would like country music.

"Saddle up"! Holiday quietly got in line as the platoon began its night patrol. The sun was setting. The land took on an eerie yellowish glow. "Hey gyrene," Holiday heard from behind him. Turning he saw a rather grizzled marine behind him, in formation, perhaps 2 or 3 years older than he. "Did you remember to go before we left? This is going to be a long trip and I don't want to have to stop for you to go to the bathroom." They both chuckled at his lame joke and continued on, as the sky got darker.

It was a hot humid night. Even though the sun had set, it was still around 90 degrees. The platoon trudged on; walking through a small clearing with pungi stakes pointing up everywhere. Holiday was surprised to see this. He had seen booby traps with pungi stakes, but never so many in one area and never with them all sticking out of the ground about a foot. They were usually found in pits, covered with jungle debris. Holiday turned to a marine and asked if he had seen anything like this before,. The Sarge, said that the VC had put them there knowing the marines would patrol at night, the hope being that as they sprang an ambush, the marines would dive to the ground for cover, and impale themselves, which by the way, said the Sarge is why they are rushing thought this area before it got completely dark.

They had set up two ambushes with no results. The new LT was anxious for a fight it seems and had that typical impatience of a western man, or an immature one, wanting results NOW and when not getting any, would move on. Holiday could tell he must be brand new from the states.

It was nearing midnight when the LT decided he wanted his platoon to climb a very high hill. The humidity and the walking had drained most of the men. Holiday echoed a low groan coming from Miller, the LT's radioman as they looked up at what promised to be hard climb. The radios they carried got heavy and neither he nor Miller were looking forward to the ascent.

Halfway up this hill, which must have been 150 meters high with a 7-9% slope, a marine collapsed and noisily rolled down the hill. The doc was right there to tend to him.

"Who the fuck was that?" growled the LT.

"Jamison, sir" Miller whispered back.

"You tell that asshole if he is going to fag out not to make so much god damn noise." Lt retorted.

Holiday stood at attention, saluted and noisily whispered "SIR YES SIR!" Holiday could feel the glare from the funewgy officer in the darkness. LT looked away and said to his radioman "Miller, give me some of your water. I ran out." Holiday smirked as Miller looked at him hesitating to share his canteen with the lieutenant.

"SIR!" Holiday whispered hoarsely, "Here you can have some of mine, I have plenty"

"Holiday I told you if you came out with 2 canteens I would have your ass."

"Yes, sir, you did. I do not have 2 canteens, sir, I have 3...plenty of water.... want some?"

In response the lieutenant, turned and began hiking up the hill. Holiday winked at Miller and Miller concealed a broad smile, while he gave the retreating LT the finger behind his back.

Finally the patrol made it to the top of the hill. The lieutenant ordered a bivouac for the night. *So much for all night ambushes*, thought Holiday. Holiday overheard the LT asking others for water and he again offered water to him.

"Get out of my sight" ordered the officer.

Holiday made arrangements with the patrol that every two hours whoever was on watch would wake him up. Each time they did, he would wake up the LT and offer him water. The LT threatened him with a court martial, but what would be the charge, offering water to a dehydrated officer? Holiday explained that the patrol was concerned with his health and did not want to have him medevacked out like the other dehydrated marine was. After all, he was their leader and the patrol would be lost without his ..."leadership"

Holiday made a lot of friends that night. They all thought he was nuts, and perhaps he was, for harassing the lieutenant.

Holiday had been formulating an attitude that most people in positions of authority abused their power, depending on the power of the position in lieu of the character of the leader. When one spends a lot of time alone, in thought, ideas do form. Holiday although young, only 19, was a bright man. He depended on empirical evidence in lieu of formal theories to draw these conclusions. A war situation creates intensity in every facet of life, in stark contrast to the boredom that one experiences. Holiday was to discover that attitudes formed in combat situations would be with him, in some cases haunt him the rest of his life.

> 25 June:67 My 19th birthday. Big deal. My birthday wish is that I make it to my 20th. By then I will be out of this hell hole. The only thing I treasured was stolen from me today. Happy fucking birthday. At least we were back on our own hill.

Holiday had spent the night before on night ambushes. He and Charlie had returned to Hill 52, the next morning after that all night patrol off of Hill 41, with that funewgy lieutenant. He was tired, and filthy from wading through rice paddies and ponds and crawling around in mud and dirt all night. The pond at the bottom of the hill was the community bath tub. The Marines claimed the north side of the pond where the village water buffalo claimed the south. After waking from a 4 hour nap, he decided to take a bath.

Any time a Marine left the hill, he carried his weapon

with him, even if it was to buy local fruit from the villagers or get a haircut from the old man who had set up a bamboo shack just outside the entrance to the hill. There was always an armed guard at the pond to watch over the bathing Marines and protect their gear as they bathed.

It was about 1030 hours and already the temperature was around 100 degrees. That water looked very inviting. Holiday stripped down, putting his watch, wallet and high school ring inside his boot. His .45, holster and belt was rolled up and placed on top of his boots. Local boys had brought the waterbo down to the pond to cool off. Many of these boys would come to the Marine's side of the pond begging for money, candy or offering to watch their possessions, for a price.

One such boy offered to watch his gear as he stood there naked. Holiday ignored him and waded into the pond. Ahhhhhhhhh that felt good. Using his bar of soap he scrubbed his entire body and slowly submerged himself to wash off the soap. As he emerged from the pond he noticed his .45 was no longer on top of his boots. By the time he reached his boots the hot sun had dried him off. Looking inside, he discovered his watch and ring were gone. With the guard nearby, Holiday surmised the kid had not risked taking the wallet with the Vietnamese money inside. He only had time enough to snatch the ring and watch. Damn!

The watch was a very expensive Seiko, he had bought at the PX in Norfolk, where he had gone to radio school, but he missed the ring far more than he did the watch.

Things had gotten so bad at home that he had quit school in April 1966 to join the Marines. But he was so smart that even with no credit for his 4th quarter in his senior year; his school had given him a diploma. His brother had gone up to the podium on graduation day and accepted his diploma on his behalf. His ring, which he had paid for, before he had quit school was given to his brother at the same time, with the message to "Tell your brother good luck in the Marines" For Holiday, that ring was recognition that even though he had quit school, he was deserving of a diploma. Holiday took great comfort in knowing that his diploma infuriated his step mother.

Sixteen years later, after getting his degree and certification as a teacher, he received a phone call from a police officer from Macon, Georgia. At the time of the call, Holiday was teaching at a school in Alabama. The police officer asked for verification of his name, the high school he had graduated from and had he had his initials engraved on the inside of his high school ring. YES!

"My name is officer George Montgomery and I found your ring in a VC bunker in Vietnam in October of

1968" "I was a tunnel rat. When I told my police chief that I had that ring and had wondered if the ring had been taken off a dead American or if it was just lost, he told me that I was a police officer, to investigate and find out. So I did"

But on June 25th, 1967 Holiday was convinced he would never see his most treasured possession ever again. Somehow that former tunnel rat had not only traced the origin of the ring but was able to discover what had happened to him after discharge from the Marine Corps.

> 21 July: 67 19 Now by almost a month. Saw a true act of courage the other night. Tatum, a black rifleman, stood in the middle of a rice paddy, with tracers flying all around in, bringing in a night medevac for a buddy. I couldn't do that. Just stand there waiting to get shot. If I had his balls I would have shot the LT for his stupidity in getting Tatum's buddy wounded. How do these assholes get to be officers? I thought marine training would have screened out a dickhead like Lt Krabb.

Holiday was exhausted after a full day humping in the heat and humidity. He welcomed the sun going down and having a slight breeze stir up the heavy air. He and Charlie had found a long tree log lying near the edge of a paddy to lean against. They figured if the VC hit them they could use either side of the log for cover.

Lt Krabb could be heard grumbling about something. Holiday didn't like Krabb. He was one of those 90-day wonders, all Mickey Mouse and no esprit de corps. Holiday could tell Krabb was scared.

"Hand me your M–79" Holiday heard Krabb say. "I'll wake his ass up" Both he and Charlie turned around to see what Krabb was up to. They saw the lieutenant raise the grenade launcher to his shoulder and pop a round towards where one of the LPs had set up. "My god" Charlie whispered, he just shot at our own guys!"

Holiday could see the explosion as it hit near the LP. Shortly afterward the LP had crawled back to the CP.

"That round blew off Johnson's leg, the marine whispered hoarsely. "I don't see how the gooks knew we were there"

"Why the fuck didn't you answer your radio, marine?" the LT whispered back.

Even in the darkness, Holiday could see the look of shock and then hate from that marine when he realized it was the LT who had fired off that round.

"Our fucking radio is out SIR" the words dripped with contempt.

After a short pause, the LT inquired, "Didn't you check the radio before you were sent out there?"

Holiday could recognize this as a transfer of responsibility from the LT to the marine as a justification for his rash and irresponsible act, which caused the loss of a man's leg. Holiday would see this tactic used repeatedly as a civilian in the public school education industry; the transference of responsibility and blame onto a teacher from a principal or department head, or onto a teacher aide from a teacher. His contempt for the lieutenant matched or surpassed that of the LP leader's.

Without orders, the LT's radioman had been on the horn calling in a medevac chopper. It could now be heard in the distance headed towards them. The radioman was giving directions and trying to pinpoint the location. Tatum, a friend of the man injured, said" I will go out and bring the chopper into the LZ.

"I didn't give you orders to............"

But Tatum was already securing two red lensed flashlights from the gunny and heading towards the field.

"The quicker we can get him medevacked out of here the better, "snorted the gunny. "Besides, you can't fault a man for showing initiative."

Holiday watched Tatum crouch towards the selected LZ while the radioman stayed on the horn guiding the chopper in. Holiday watched as Tatum stood up in the gloom, two red beams from his flashlights searching the night sky; and he saw something else which made his blood run cold.......tracer rounds, coming from 3 sides, aimed right at Tatum. The gooks were all around them.

Holiday busied himself getting the wounded man on a poncho. Then he and 3 others picked up the corners and carried the man to the edge of the paddy. Holiday watched Tatum scrunch his shoulders as if doing so would keep him protected from the bullets being fired at him. He saw Tatum cross the lights in Standard Operating Procedure, guiding the chopper down. He could swear Tatum's eyes were closed. On signal, the 4 Marines stumbled out into the paddy with their wounded comrade. Holiday had handed the severed leg to the wounded Marine. Placing it on his chest until the wounded man had clutched it with both hands, shouted over the din of the chopper blades, "Here, this is yours".

Holiday saw 2 men jump out of the chopper even before the chopper landed carrying a stretcher.

Within seconds, the stretcher had been transferred under the body and now the men were each carrying a handle and rushing towards the waiting helicopter. Holiday had the lighter end, the end with only one leg, the stump bleeding through the compress doc had put on with the lower limb of the severed leg clumsily put on top of the body. Holiday was not sure if the wounded man was holding his leg to keep it from falling off the stretcher or not.

Before he knew it, they were upon the chopper. Holiday raised his end of the stretcher. The gunner inside the hatch was pulling on the upper half of the stretcher. In horror Holiday watched him drop his end from a height of 3 feet and over the din of the chopper's blade heard the scream from his wounded comrade. In a rage and on impulse, Holiday reached up and grabbing the gunner by his ankle dragged him out of the hatch. While the two who had brought the stretcher to him scrambled back on board, Holiday screamed into the gunners face, "Are you scared marine?"

"You don't treat this man like a piece of meat. You can stay with us tonight, ALL night and we will see how scared you can get."

The marine pilot took off quickly. Holiday did not know if the others had seen him pull a marine off the chopper or not, but he was so angry he did not care. Grabbing the scared marine by his collar and walking back to relative safety, Holiday shouted in his ear, "You are scared for 10 seconds flyboy. We are scared all the time. Maybe if you spend the night with us, you will grow enough balls to treat our wounded buddies with more respect."

Oblivious to Holiday were the tracers flying all around him. Tatum ran up to him screaming

"Are you crazy? Let's get OUT of here."

Ironic that Tatum would call him crazy, after seeing Tatum stand in the middle of a rice paddy with two lit flashlights that acted like magnets for bullets, guiding that chopper into a hot LZ. Curious, that men cannot see their own bravery............or stupidity as the case may be.

Within seconds they were back with the rest of the patrol. Holiday could hear the gunny shouting at him, to get his ass over to him and to bring that flyboy with him.

"Just what do you think you are doing hauling this useless piece of shit flyboy over here?" asked the gunny. "We are gonna have to feed him, wipe his ass when he shits, listen to him cry all damn night, calling for his mama....."

Tatum, rather than Holiday explained what the door gunner had done. It was Tatum's buddy that had been wounded and Tatum was grateful that Holiday had done what he had done. Holiday was dismissed. The LT had said nothing, perhaps too ashamed to, given the fact that he was the cause of this incident in the first place.

After about 10 minutes the gunny called him over. *Shit, he is going to tell me I am gonna get busted for this.*

"Holiday" The gunny started, "Well done, but don't you ever pull a stupid stunt like that again, or I will have your ass in a sling for the duration, you got that?"

Holiday could not help grin in relief. "Yes gunny, it won't happen again".

As he turned to crawl back to his position, he felt a hand on his shoulder. "Thanks man" he heard Tatum say. Holiday was a bit surprised. Tatum was black and a bit of a racist. His buddy who lost the leg was black and also didn't like whites. As Holiday grunted, then started to crawl back, he thought to himself *The only two colors out here are green (the uniform) and red (the blood)*

"Tatum" Holiday whispered over his shoulder, "We all bleed red"

As he sat next to Charlie, he felt a nudge from his buddy. Looking at him, Holiday saw him nod and grunt, then a whisper in his ear. "For a white boy you alright" and a chuckle.

> *28 July:* 67 Got attacked by red ants today. They must be commies, they are red aren't they? I hate these bugs, red scorpions, black scorpions, yellow and red 13 inch centipedes, poisonous at that. Snakes, bamboo vipers called Two -steps, once bitten, two steps later and you are dead. Blood sucking slugs, Rats as big as small cats and now ants that bite!

It had been a hot day. The squad had been on a long day patrol, in an unfamiliar area. The patrol had gone west and north from the hill. This was very close to Army Special Forces' TAOR (tactical area of responsibility). The sun was starting to set and it had cooled down to the low 90's. Jefferson, the point man had led the patrol South and West up a hill where the vegetation had been stunted, by agent orange. There were bushes and shrubs no higher than 8 feet. On the slope one could look southeast and see Hill 52, no more than a mile away. Holiday guessed Jefferson was arcing back in a huge circle towards the hill, but where they were gave them a good view of the entire area; foot hills to the North, rice paddies due East in the direction of the hill, the river to the South and the sun and mountains due West where the Green Berets had a compound and 600 CIDG men (militia).

Holiday saw Jefferson raise his hand in a signal to stop. Automatically, every Marine either knelt or squatted, to lower their profile so as not to be a target. Jefferson waved for Cpl Owens to come up to point. After a minute of discussion, Owens waved for the whole squad to join him. That was very unusual for any squad leader to motion for the entire squad to bunch up, especially in unfamiliar territory.

As Holiday got closer, he saw why. There was a column of ants heading from West to East cutting off the Marines effort to travel South by Southeast. It was like a wall of red for as far as one could see, traveling down the hill towards the village and rice paddies. This wall stretched from the ground to the highest branches on the stunted shrubbery. With less than an hour of daylight left, there was no way around them. The Marines would have to go through them.

The Marines crowded around Owens. "We gotta go through these motherfuckers. Roll your sleeves down, blouse your boots, button all buttons and keep your helmet on your dome" he ordered everyone. "Jeff and Wiff, you two go through first, beat the ants off of each other and then I will send one guy at a time. These motherfuckers hurt. Now cover up good"

Holiday watched each man go through. As each gyrene ran through the wall of red, he could see the ants leap from all sides on each man. It was a strange site. Literally hundreds of nasty mean red ants jumping from all levels to attack the men in green. Holiday watched each man then get beat with several hands trying to knock off all the attackers. They would have to back away from the column to avoid another attack. The ants would orient themselves and return to the column in the relentless desire to head East, down the hill. All of them had made it through. Holiday was the last to go. He made sure all his buttons were buttoned and with the radio still on his back, he rushed through the angry ants, using his hands to shield his eyes and face. As he ran through, he saw hundreds of ants leave their perches on the leaves and branches and jump towards him. He could feel them land on his body and he swore later that he could hear them hissing in anger at him that he would dare disrupt their migration.

Once on the other side, he saw several Marines slapping at him, someone had ripped his radio off his back to rid it of the ants. After hundreds of slaps and whacks, it was over. Then suddenly Holiday doubled over in pain. Somehow one of those ants had penetrated his defenses and had gotten inside his crotch area and had bitten him on his scrotum. Holiday dug inside his trousers, found that murderous bastard and squeezed him to death amid a chorus of snickers and chuckles from his comrades. "Seems like that little fucker wanted your family jewels, Holiday", someone cried out. More snickers.

"Let's head home," ordered Owens. "Jefferson my man, lead us homeward". Someone from the rear says "Hey Holiday was it good for you, too"? Chuckles. "That commie ant wanted you, man" More chuckles and laughter. Holiday hated these damn bugs.

> 13 Aug: 67 just got back from a week- long operation. We finally went after those damn gooks on the other side of the river. About time. It got nasty for a while, some marines bought it. I had to pistol whip a lifer on the third day when we got pinned down in that trench. Arty LT saw me do it too and never said a word about it to me. That lifer bastard was spreading panic with all his whining. I had to shut him up. Ran into a regiment of NVA on that day. Those bastards didn't hit and run. They duked it out with us all day and we had two tanks. But they had RPGs and B-40 rockets.

Charlie ripped back the poncho that was doubling as a hatch to Holidays two man hooch. Holiday and he had just gotten off an all-night ambush patrol and Holiday was still sleeping when Charlie barged in.

"Yo dude, got some skinny for you. We go out on an operation tomorrow"

"No shit," Holiday responded", an operation...must be big...what's the objective?"

"Do I look like the captain to you?" "Look, Look, "continued Charlie, "I know where we are going and you and I need to set up some fire missions, you know, go over coordinates and shit."

"Where we going?" asked Holiday. "In 7 o'clock Charlie's back yard" smiled Charlie.

Holiday bolted up from his rack, "You mean, right across the river?"

"Yeah, smiled Charlie, "Arizona Territory." "Those VC been harassing us long enough".

Charlie and Holiday had been on plenty of patrols, setting up night, and day ambushes. The reason his unit had been sent to this hill was to destroy the supply line the VC were using in the area. From what the Captain had told them, there was an offshoot of the Ho Chi Min trail that they suspected crossed the river somewhere close to this hill.

There had been several times when patrols had caught

the VC humping supplies. Charlie and Holiday had become very important to these patrols since they represented the "artillery" firepower. Hill 52 was too far from Hill 65 where two batteries of 155 and 105 Howitzers had been assigned. As a team, Charlie and Holiday had been responsible for nearly 100 kills in the past few months. They knew they had been effective in at least slowing down the supply traffic throughout their region of I Corps. This was confirmed by the number of snipers, booby traps, leaflets identifying their unit and promising death to all, the constant fire fights when they were on patrol, the probes at night testing their defenses, the night mortar attacks, and the slowdown of supplies feeding into the VC complex in their region.

Holiday felt that they were doing their job well enough to make a dent in whatever strategy that was running this war. And now, finally, they were taking it to the enemy in a force larger than a platoon or a squad or fire team.

The next morning Holiday and Charlie boarded an Amtrack. These vestiges of WWII looked like a shoebox on treads. They sat inside the guts of this thing for what seemed like hours. Then they felt it begin to move, a slow rumble, lurching the 12 bodies back and forth as it lumbered across the shallow river. Above the din of the engine Holiday could hear the PING PING of bullets bouncing off the outer armor of the amphibian behemoth. A few more lurches, PINGs and after a few more minutes, the hatches gave way, facing back towards the river.

Gunny was at the open hatch yelling "GO" "GO", and waving to the direction he wanted the marines to go. Everyone stumbled out and after a second or so of disorientation, headed towards a distant tree line, right into the jaws of the incoming small arms fire.

Charlie and Holiday dove for the same tree, hearts pumping but glad to still be alive. After a few more minutes, the order to "move out" was given. Minutes later, they came upon a few hooches, not a vil, but some other Marines had already caught some POWS. Holiday and Charlie were assigned to watch over them. Through sporadic fire and long minutes of silence, the two Marines chatted about the young man and the older man, and wondered why these people hated the US so much. Didn't they know we were here to save them from Communism?

Vietnamese do not sit on the ground as Americans do. They squat on their haunches. The one POW kept staring at them with intense hate in his eyes, while the older of the 2 kept his eyes on the ground. Charlie offered water and crackers from his C rat pack to the one with the hate filled eyes. He just kept glaring at the 2 Marines.

The Marines had taken a Vietnamese interpreter with them on this operation. He called himself Sgt Flowers.

"Him VC" Sgt Flowers said as he approached them. Holiday had been part of other sessions questioning POW s and knew what to do, especially with Sgt. Flowers. Flowers looked like a boy, no older than he was; but Flowers was ruthless in his tactics. The story was that the VC had killed his father in front of him as a way to intimidate the villagers. His hate for the VC was ...intense.

Flowers squatted in front of the younger man whose eyes radiated with hate. This was going to be an interesting session. Holiday squatted to the right of Flowers and took out his K-bar and began toying with it. Flowers began the interrogation, the prisoner remained silent. The Vietnamese had the habit of putting their hands together when under duress or feeling stress, especially when squatting, they cupped their hands together in front of their face. This young prisoner was no exception, but over his clasped hands he continued to glare with intense hate. Holiday stuck his K-bar in the dirt and with one quick move grabbed both hands and yanked them apart and with a deliberate and forceful motion, placed the hands on the knees of the POW. The glare instantly was directed towards him. Holiday kept a stoic expression.

Flowers kept up his tirade asking question after question. Eventually the POW brought his hands together covering his mouth. Holiday instantly grabbed both hands by the wrists and repeated his previous actions. Again, the glare of hate.

The reason for doing this was to distract the prisoner, intimidate him and get him to answer a question before he could get his defenses up. After several repetitions of this tactic, Sgt Flowers said in English, "This is not working". Holiday picked up his K-bar, and ran the flat side of it along the cheek of the young man. "Ask now Sarge", Holiday said. Flowers began his tirade of questions, using feigned anger in his voice to elicit a response. Holiday turned the blade towards the cheek and made a slow but superficial cut along his cheek. The POW just glared with the same intense hate.

The older man started jabbering away.

"What's he saying" inquired Holiday.

Flowers answered, "He say boy his son, no cut him. He say he will answer any questions."

Holiday grinned. Keeping the blade on the young man's cheek, Flowers began interrogating the father....... getting answers to all his questions. Sgt Flowers, asked "Old man want to know will you kill him now?"

"NO" Holiday snorted. "We got what we wanted". Both men settled back, waiting for someone to take these 2 VC POW s from them.

After about an hour the order was given to move

out again. A grunt had come to escort the prisoners somewhere from the combat zone while Charlie and Holiday went to rejoin the captain and his CP group.

By now it was stifling hot and both men had taken off their flak jackets. When the order had come, they scooped up their jackets and as they exited the open stone hutch they had been in, a shot rang out and Holiday saw Pfc Ramone spin once and collapse.

Ramone held up his hand. "Shit!" "They shot my goddamn finger off"

"Charlie snorted, "It ain't your fuck finger, so quit whining about it.

Doc was on him in a heartbeat, as Ramone went into shock. "Make yourself useful Holiday and call in a medevac," Holiday heard Gunny call out.

Within minutes, the chopper was on the ground as Holiday and 3 others carried Ramone in a poncho, out to the waiting chopper. Captain had thought he had cleared the immediate area of VC, but Holiday could hear the Zings and buzzes of bullets passing all around him as Ramone was carried to the CH-34.(I have a photo, from a newspaper clipping of myself and 3 others carrying Ramone to a waiting medevac chopper, while bullets were zinging all around us. In fact, it is on the cover of this book)

The rest of the day was spent chasing the enemy up and down hills, through vils, and across rice paddies. Marines were dipping their canteens into streams not even stopping to fill them up but scooping up whatever water they could by trolling the canteens. Coming through one vil, many Marines, Holiday included, were hacking un-ripe pineapples from their stalks, cutting off the prickly skins as they walked, more for the juice than the meat, since no one had eaten since 0500 that morning. But they were more thirsty than hungry.

By 1400, almost a dozen Marines had been medevacked out for heat strokes. Holiday wound up carrying an M 79 grenade launcher along with his .45 caliber pistol and his radio. The Marines had forced every VC in the area through a blocking force of 600 CIDG men commanded by a Special Forces team. The enemy went through them like a sieve.

That night, the temperature went down to 70 degrees Fahrenheit. Holiday had to share a poncho with another Marine to stay warm. Funny thing. Shivering in 70 degrees.

The next morning, the company expected to return to their hills and bases, but there had been a call for a "bald eagle". A "bald eagle" was a company strength rescue mission. A "sparrow hawk" was a platoon sized rescue mission. A "CAP" unit had been hit the previous night. The Marines had fought off the attack, with one casualty but had used up all their ammo.

Holiday and Charlie were not sure where they were going but they knew they were going too far for 81 mortars to be effective. Charlie asked the captain if he and Holiday could return to Hill 52 but the captain said no, there was no way for them to return. Disappointed, the both climbed aboard the already hot to the touch Amtrak. They had to tough it out until their fannies got used to the heat, but at least they were not going to walk. It was a nice break from grunting it on the ground.

The company rode all afternoon and into early evening, before ordered to halt. They set up bivouac in a crescent shaped sand bar, which, at one time had been a bend in the nearby river they had come to.

The next morning, the CP group was in a huddle trying to figure out where they were. Holiday sidled up and pointed on the map and said "Here Sir" The gunny glared at him and said something like, "does the lance corporal think he is smarter than the officers or the gunny for that matter"? This incident impressed Holiday. He began to see where facts and truth did not matter, but rank did i.e. who holds the power. "Might makes right" was the term he could have used.

But being only19 and trying to be helpful Holiday had done what he thought was right.

With that stinging comment from the gunny, Holiday went over to a rice paddy dike and took off his boots to scratch his feet. He had gotten jungle rot pretty bad and it made his feet itch like crazy.

While engaged in this manner, he heard a marine shout out "Hey there are troops in that vil, over there" Sure enough, Holiday could see men in green uniforms of the NVA, not the black pajamas of the VC running about within the village. "Holy Shit!" NVA! They had the reputation of staying in a battle and fighting it out, unlike the VC whose hit and run tactics were what most Marines were used to.

Gunny quickly ordered his 60mm mortars set up. Holiday and Charlie felt useless. They were nowhere near any friendly hill with 81mm mortars. Charlie had an older M14 rifle while Holiday had only a .45 automatic pistol. Gunny had the 60mm guns pumping out rounds while the captain was ordering the company to move forward. Holiday still had his boots off. Scrambling to get them back on and laced, he heard Charlie shout to him, "Let's go".

Charlie headed towards the firing, running alongside a line of hooches on the outskirts of the vil. Holiday was right behind him, laces dragging on the ground. He jumped behind a grave mound, as that was the only thing he could use for cover. As he pulled up his legs to lace his boots, while lying on his side, he saw the dirt kicking up not more than 10 inches from his face. Holiday couldn't hide any lower that he was. Looking up he saw the gunny waving him towards a stone building. Both he and Charlie bolted towards the porch on the front of the building. There were 4 giant stone pillars acting as columns holding up the roof of this thing. Charlie got behind one of them and Holiday behind another.

Holiday looked over at his buddy. Charlie's eyes were huge from fear. Holiday always found that a bit comical, for Charlie's eyes seemingly bugging out of their sockets. As they sat there, hiding, Holiday could hear the artillery FO, Lt Simms, calling for his radioman, Stansburgh. Stansburgh was hiding alongside the wall of the huge structure. Holiday could hear the fear in his voice as he kept whimpering, "I am not going up there I have a wife and kids I don't want to die."

Holiday looked over at Charlie. The firepower was so intense that it sounded like a constant roar. There was a trench about 40 or 50 feet ahead of them where most of the marines were crouching and firing back at the NVA.

"I'll go up there, "Holiday called over to Charlie.

"No you won't, Charlie retorted.

"But the LT needs a radio and Stansburgh is too fucking scared to."

"You ain't going up there, Holiday".

Holiday got angry and yelled back, "Why the fuck not?"

"Cuz if you die," Charlie responded, "I gotta carry that damn radio".

Holiday burst out laughing. Charlie's face was so serious when he said that, but it struck him funny that he was more concerned with carrying the radio than the safety of his partner. Charlie began to laugh along with Holiday

"That mother fucker is heavy, laughed Charlie "and I ain't gonna carry that damn thing, not as hot as its been, so you stay alive, mother fucker". They both laughed again.

After a few more minutes, the shooting had stopped. They both made a run for the trenches, as only a few sporadic rounds were shot their way. Both sides, it seemed had paused to assess their situation and plan some strategy. Holiday had jumped into the trench next to LT Simms, thinking he could use his radio for calling in fire missions. But before he could change the frequency over to the artillery one, Stansburgh had leaped into the trench between the LT and Holiday. This seemed to trigger the firefight. All hell broke loose again.

On one side of Holiday, a black Marine was breathing rapidly and sweating profusely. On the other was Stansburgh, his elbows and knees on the ground and his ass sticking up in the air, sobbing like baby. LT looked at Holiday then at Stansburgh with disgust.

"I, I, I'm scared" the black man stuttered. "I ain't been this scared in my whole life."

"Look" Holiday grunted, "You got at least 4 inches from the top of the trench to your head. Bullets don't drop down, they fly over you. So as long as you don't poke your head up, you will be ok, so sit and relax and listen to the war go by".

The young black stared at him incredulously.

"Ain't you scared?"

Holiday stared back and nodded, "Hell yes I'm scared, but ya can't show it, you gotta function, do your job, cuz the other guys are counting on you." "You can't fall apart like Stansburgh here", he shouted over the din, pointing at the man still crying and whimpering about not wanting to die. So they sat, that rifleman, Holiday, and LT, with Stansburgh kneeling with his face in the dirt. *"Maybe that isn't crying about not wanting to die. Maybe he is praying,"* thought Holiday.

Just then, the black marine screamed, in the highest pitched scream Holiday has ever heard come out of a man's mouth, "**A grenade, what do I do**?" Holiday reached down, picked up the chicom (an acronym for Chinese Communist) grenade and as he pitched it back out of the trench, he shouted, "You throw it back, asshole" As he threw it, he could hear Stansburgh, losing it, AH, AH ,AH, AH in a shrill voice. The grenade exploded not 10 feet from the trench. His arm had hit the side of the trench and jarred the grenade lose from his grip. "Shut the fuck up," Holiday screamed, as he pulled his pistol out of its holster, "Shut up or I'll shut you up"

Holiday knew Stansburgh's antic could start a wave of panic. If that happened it would be like signing a death warrant. The Marines would quit functioning as a fighting unit, and the NVA could be emboldened enough to attack their position, possibly over run it.

Holiday grabbed Stansburgh by the back of his collar and yanking him up from the mud, proceeded to pistol whip that man about the head and shoulders, until the hysterical screaming stopped. Looking over at the LT on the other side of Stansburgh, Lt said, "I saw nothing" Then, "I have a fire mission to call in, can you handle the call in?"

"Yes Sir" yelled, Holiday.

For the next hour, marines and NVA soldiers tried throwing grenades into each other's trench line. LT's fire mission finally had the NVA breaking and running.

The rounds landed so close that the ground shook, the trench shook, the water in the trench made ripples. You could feel the blast of air from the concussion of the rounds hitting the ground.

Unlike the movies, where in a charge everyone cheers and leaps out of the trench, when the order was given to advance, no cheer, no "let's do this for god and country" just a company of mostly young men in their late teens and early 20's, crawling out of the mud, with rifles firing and grenades being thrown.

There had been 2 tanks assigned to the company for this operation. When the fire fight started, neither tank would advance. Holiday discovered later that the NVA had B-40 rockets, tank killers, and had fired at the tanks well in the rear of the fight.

With the advance of the troops, the tanks moved up rather quickly to support the grunts. The marines moved, almost jogged through the trees and bush and around hutches as the NVA retreated in front of them, firing back at the marines as they melted into the jungle.

Holiday saw a marine, clutching his stomach, calling for his mama, with a look of utter surprise and shock on his face. He turned towards Holiday, taking his hands away from his guts, Holiday saw the man's intestines fall into his now cupped hands just below the belt line. "Look" the marine said, then "MAMA" then with his eyes rolling into the back of his head, he collapsed. Holiday kept moving forward. He knew there was nothing he could have done for that man.

Within a few minutes, the entire company had broken into a clearing inside the center of the vil. The vil and the jungle around them had gone deathly quiet after the noise of war they had experienced the past several hours. It was eerie. Holiday knelt behind a bush and puked his guts out. The site of that man holding his intestines and calling for his mother was too much.

Holiday stood up, a bit dizzy, looking for Charlie. He saw him coming towards him, "Yo Holiday, the captain wants to use you as a tunnel rat…" "You ok?" Charlie had noticed the green pallor on Holidays face. "Some fire fight, eh Holiday, Charlie queried. Charlie had a habit of talking real fast and trying to come up with funny stuff to say, after a firefight .It was his way to get over his fear and deal with what he had just experienced. "And I see I don't have to carry that fucking radio, he snickered". Holiday forced a grin and said, "Nope, not today" and moved up to see what the captain wanted from him.

Holiday was a thin man, boy really, barely 19, standing 6'1, but only about 150 pounds, skinny enough to crawl through VC tunnels, apparently. Approaching the captain, Holiday, grunted "Skipper"? "Well, Holiday, you were complaining you had nothing to do being out of range for 81 support, so I thought I'd volunteer you for tunnel rat duty. You up for it?" Holiday cringed inside. "Yes Sir" "Ok then, go with gunny, and he'll show you where you are going in. You come back alive and tell us what you see in there, got that Marine? "Yes Sir" Holiday replied. Just then he saw a Marine drag a dead body out from a tunnel entrance. It was a very old woman.

Holiday was guided towards one of the tunnel openings. With guts churning Holiday began crawling inside. In one hand he held his .45 and in the other, a flashlight. He thought that stupid. The enemy would be able to see his light long before his light could expose where they were. He clicked it off and crawled along, depending solely on his hearing. He would pause now and then and listen……………..nothing. Then crawl some more, stop and listen.

After about 15 minutes of this, Holiday could feel a change in the structure of the pitch-black tunnel. He sensed a chamber or an opening. He tried to regulate his breathing so if anyone were there ahead of him in the dark they would not hear him. He began to inch forwards slowly and quietly. He felt the edge of the end of the wall he had been following. He could sense a chamber ahead of him and to the left. It was pitch black. Slowing he crawled forward…… BOO! Holidays heart leapt into this throat He rolled on his back and pointed his .45 at the noise. Then he heard a chuckle. "Scared ya didn't I" laughed the other tunnel rat. "I almost shot you, asshole" Holiday shot back.

"Well I didn't know who you were until I smelled you" I almost shot you too"

"You smelled me?"

"Yup" whispered the marine. "You smelled like a grunt, not like a gook."

You can tell the difference" queried Holiday?

"Sure, can't you?"

They sat for a long time saying nothing. Both reflecting on the events of the day, each lost in his own vivid and graphic memories. Finally the grunt spoke up. "Well, let's go tell the skipper we didn't find anything here" "But I bet other rats did in other places."

The firefight had started early in the morning, but it was now late afternoon. The Marines were exhausted but glad that it was over. After setting up a perimeter and putting out LPs (listening posts) Holiday found a tree to sit against. It was starting to cool down; the sun was now below the trees that bordered the town "square".

Out of nowhere Holiday heard a voice say, "There ain't no Yankee bad enough to kick my ass". Disgusted with the stupid remark being voiced after a day of fighting

NVA, Holiday retorted, "This Yankee can". The redneck Marine stood up and motioning to Holiday, said, "Well come on, Yankee". Holiday, still leaning against the tree, pulled out his .45 and his K bar, and said softly, "So...... what's it gonna be, guns or knives"?

Out of nowhere came the Gunny's voice.

"SIT DOWN, Alabama"

"But gunny, the redneck replied, "This Yankee thinks he is bad news".

Gunny, in a loud voice, responded, "He is from New York. They don't play. Sit down."

Then turning to Holiday ordered him to holster his weapon. As Holiday put away his K bar and .45, he saw Gunny put his nose on the other Marine's nose and whisper, " I said sit DOWN you numbnuts, shit for brains."

The rest of the evening and night passed without incident".

> 28 Aug: 67 Charlie was killed today. I puked all afternoon. Charlie was a shortimer, less than 30 days. He died saving my life. I feel so bad. I am angry, bitter. I want to kill all these bastards. I can't write any more.

It was hot. They had been patrolling for hours. One platoon, on a search and destroy patrol. These patrols were done daily and were actually done for two main reasons: to seek out and destroy the enemy and to insure there has been no evidence of enemy troop movement against them. Holiday had gotten used to the daily grind He preferred to be out in the bush patrolling rather than back on the hill doing nothing or engaging in some useless activity to keep the troops busy. At least on patrol holiday felt he was doing something important. He and Charlie were the "artillery" support for the grunts, in the form of 81 mortars. If anything happened, the grunts would turn to them to call in 81 rounds. Many times it had tipped a firefight in their favor.

Holiday never did fully understand the strategy being employed by the top brass. Did the top brass really think that patrolling a 5000-yard perimeter each day was going to uncover any major enemy activity? Hell they had been on so many patrols in this area that they began to give the locals nicknames. There was gramps, which liked to play "slapsies" with the guys and that old fart usually won too. There was Bun and his gang of younger kids always playing a Vietnamese version of cowboys and Indians or cops and robbers. There was gramma-son, a very old woman who tended to her garden religiously and had a penchant for American cigarettes, preferably Marlboros. There was the cute 14-year-old girl, the guys called Amy. Who knows how she got dubbed an American name, probably reminded one of the guys of his kid sister. Even at the age of 14, she stirred up lust in the hearts of most of the horny marines, but although she was talked about no one ever tried to make a move on her. But she was knock out gorgeous.

The patrol had moved through a vil and was cutting across a rice paddy. It was still the dry season and the paddies were low on water. Several paddies had low small hills, more like mounds or dirt in the middle. Many of these mounds were used to shuck the rice. The locals used wide, shallow bamboo weaved baskets. One of these mounds had several strewn around as the patrol approached.

Doc calls out, "I am getting me one of them for shade. It is fucking HOT."

"Don't do it," Charlie called back. "It might be booby trapped."

"Oh, hell Charlie, it's not going to be booby trapped. It is noontime and they all went back to the vil for chow and to get out of the heat of the day."

"Leave it be. Don't be stupid," Charlie replied.

"Doc, leave it," shouted Holiday. "Fuck you jarhead," doc shouted over his shoulder as he jogged towards the biggest one. Doc was about 4 paces ahead and to the left of Charlie, who was a pace ahead of Holiday. This corpsman was not the same one who had bandaged up Holiday when those two other marines had gotten medevacked from stepping on a trip wire. This one was new to the outfit.

Charlie was eyeing him keenly, still yelling at the doc to leave it be. Holiday noticed that the yelling had gotten the lieutenant's attention. As the LT glanced back over his shoulder, doc picked up the bamboo basket. The explosion was loud. Holiday felt a tug on his back as a piece of shrapnel whizzed past his ear and knocked off his antenna from the radio. "Charlie, look at…." Charlie was in a heap 2 feet in front of Holiday. Holiday saw blood, so much blood… He immediately sat on the ground and cradled Charlie's head in his lap. He saw that half of Charlie's face had been blown off and his chest was open and gushing blood. There was no need to call the doc since the doc was dead. With a sinking feeling muddled with an intense love for his friend, Holiday realized that to save him, his friend had jumped in front of the explosion, that both knew what would happen if doc tried to pick up that basket.

"You stupid mother fucker, why did you do it, why did you….?" Through a gaping hole where Charlie's teeth and mouth had been, Holiday heard Charlie gurgle, "Someone has to care …" He never finished his sentence. Holiday heard the death rattle and watched as Charlie's eyes moved up to the top of his head, in a death stare, seeing nothing. The blood continued to gush from the chest wound and from his face.

By then the entire patrol was circled around Holiday as he rocked Charlie's body, like a mother would a baby as she cooed to try and get the baby to sleep. But what the marines heard was a low anguished cry coming from the soul of Holiday that ended in a wail of agony.

Holiday did not remember gentle hands pulling him away from Charlie's body, nor did he remember the chopper landing and picking up the remains of a dead marine and navy corpsman. Holiday had been left on his own as the rest of the patrol did what needed to be done to fly out the bodies and secure the area from possible ambush. Many times, the enemy would be very close to booby traps, to spring an ambush in the confusion that followed a casualty from a booby trap, but not this time.

The Lieutenant walked up to Holiday and asked, "You gonna be ok?"

Holiday looked into LT's eyes and snarled, "Yes sir".

LT took a closer look, then turned to a grunt and said, "Take your fire team and escort this Marine back to the hill". Holiday glared at him. "You are no good to me Marine with no FO, humping a radio that you cannot use and having only a .45. I don't want you getting ideas to 'borrow' a rifle again," he said with a smile as he patted Holiday's arm. Holiday did not smile back. "Corporal McCall was a good marine, and I know he was your friend, but you are in no shape to continue, marine and I don't want to lose any more good men. Now head back to the hill and report to HQ and let them know what happened here."

"Aye aye, sir" Holiday muttered as he headed back to the hill. Holiday did not look for booby-traps, did not scan the jungle for VC, he just walked back to the hill in a daze not caring for his own life, but agonizing over the loss of his friend. He spent the rest of the day vomiting and sleeping, lying on someone else's bunk

> 30 Aug: 67 Battalion sends me a new FO to take Charlie's place. This guy is a big white guy from Missouri. He chews tobacco. Friendly enough. His name is Goodwin. From now on I call everyone by their last name. I will not allow myself to get close to anyone again. He moved in with one of the gun crews. I still have the hooch to myself. That's OK with me. I like my privacy. With all the patrols they send me on I need to catch sleep when I can. I don't like hanging out listening to a bunch of bullshit talk anyway.

"Saddle up" Holiday hears the squad leader call. It's early morning and he and Goodwin have been ordered to go on patrol, yet again. Because this hill is so isolated, they depend on Holiday and Goodwin to be there artillery support. Hill 65 is close enough, barely for them to use the heavy stuff from the 155's but there is only one artillery FO for the battalion and he stays on Hill 65 with Kilo Company. Hill 52 depends on the 81 mortars.

Holiday is in the middle of the column as usual,

working his way down the hill, through the barbed wire and booby traps. His heart races as it always does at the beginning of a patrol. He has been on so many patrols at all hours of the day and night that he knows it is not from excitement but from fear, that his pulse quickens.

Today, they will search West and North of the hill, going into the foothills of the mountains just North of their base camp. It will be a hot one. Their job as always is to search for the enemy and destroy. But more specifically, to disrupt the supply line coming from N Vietnam as best and as often as they can. The VC usually use the trails at night, but Lima Company had been very effective at setting up ambushes and key places along the supply line, so S-2 (intelligence) had told them that there was more activity during the day.

The squad was sitting on the South side of a hill, peering out North and West, where a branch of the Ho Chi Minh trail was. It was hot, very hot. Doc, another crazy corpsman was on this patrol. Holiday started breathing hard. Doc crawls over. "What's up"?

"I don't feel so good'" Holiday muttered, " Kinda dizzy".

"Drink some water", replied the corpsman.

"Out"

"How can you be out? We have only been here an hour" Doc retorted.

"He gave all his water to Lieutenant Krabb", smirked a grunt. Everyone started to chuckle.

"Hey, Holiday," hollered the squad leader, "are you the guy that fucked with Krabb about bringing extra water?"

"He be the one", snorted a grunt.

"Where is your third canteen, forget it"?

"Hell, I forgot my second canteen, "muttered Holiday.

Goodwin, the newbie FO, crawls up to Holiday. "Here, take a swig of my water." He whispered.

"He can drink your whole canteen and it will not be enough, Johnson, why not head down to that brook, we can all use some fresh water; and no need to whisper, newbie; there is no one within a hundred yards of us" stated Doc.

So, they got their gear together, and in single file, headed down towards a rapidly flowing brook coming down from the central Highland mountains. The squad leader found a place along the brook, where it had made a pool of sorts about 12 feet in diameter and 2 ½ feet deep. Holiday walked into the pool and sat down. He filled his canteen with the clear and tasty water 3 times and drank it all.

He felt his body welcome the refreshing liquid as he felt his body respond, gaining energy and strength, the more he drank. "Don't piss in there, we are drinking too", hollered a grunt; they all laughed.

As he sat there, immersed, he reflected back to a time when, in August of his sophomore year, all the football players would get together each evening for conditioning and informal practices to get ready for the season. On one occasion, while running laps, he had gotten the same weak feeling for the same reason. He was dehydrated. Football players and sons of his father, pushed on, so he pushed on, until he began staggering, nearly fainting. Two seniors came up to him, grabbed him by his arms and slowed him down to a walk.

"This is conditioning, you do not push yourself until you die, Holiday" Come over to the pool with me, can you walk?"

There was a swimming pool right next to the quarter mile track they had been running on. Holiday half stumbled and half walked to the aid station. A lifeguard gave him all the water he wanted and then bought him a candy bar. A candy bar! Was he being rewarded for fagging out on the track? He was so confused. None of the kids in his family were allowed to eat candy. It was considered a frivolous waste of hard earned money.

And if his father ever found out he nearly fainted while attending football conditioning, he would be mocked and ridiculed by his father, being called a sissy and a quitter. He would most certainly be furious were he to find out he had candy after acting like such a sissy… Holiday savored every bite of that chocolate bar…Fuck his father.

As the cool water rushed around him, soaking into his skin and breathing new life into him, Holiday grunted to himself. He wondered if his father would scream at him and call him a sissy, for nearly fainting again. "Hey doc, got any candy bars?" Fuck his father.

19 Sept: 67 Good day today, got 17 kills.

Goodwin has turned out to be an effective FO, a little slower than Charlie was but he got the job done. Holiday knew as much about being an FO as the FO's did. He even helped train Goodwin, not only on how to call in fire missions but on how to survive in the bush.

After a couple of hours of humping up and down the foothills, the squad took a break. They were sitting atop one of the many treeless hills, that hugged the base of the mountain range, when Holiday heard a grunt say, "We got company". Immediately all the grunts ducked down. Holiday crawled over to Cpl Simms, the patrol leader. Goodwin crawled up next to him.

There below them coming down the hill in front of

them was a line of VC carrying sacks and crates. Holiday could not help but think that had they not stopped to rest, they would have been in that valley with the VC peering down at them, instead.

Cpl Simms leans towards Holiday and asks, "Ya think you can fuck em up from here?"

"Well," Goodwin answered, "We are still within range for 81's, don't you think Holiday?" The patrol leaders had gotten used to working with Holiday rather than any newbie FO or "Funewgy" (fucking new guy) as the grunts called the new people in the company. Holiday didn't mind Goodwin answering. After all he was the FO. Holiday was merely the radioman.

"Hell yeah," Holiday replied. Goodwin pulled out his map, finds the coordinates and gives them to Holiday. Each map had certain checkpoints located where grid lines crossed on the maps. These grid lines were given names and used as primary reference points when calling in fire missions. "Whisky Lima, this is Lima Forward, Fire mission," Holiday barked into the PRC25 radio. "From Orange, from Orange, right 200, down 450, one round H E."

Goodwin as FO was supposed to choose what type of rounds to use and in most cases; a white phosphorous round was used as a marker then fire was adjusted from that mark. But Holiday had such a clear view from the vantage point of the hill that he chose an H E (high explosive) round as a marker.

Hill 52 had two 81 mortars, as did every company in the battalion. Two guns could be very effective when working in tangent on a fire mission if the gun crews were good and Lima Company's gun crews were very good.

Within a minute, the first round landed a little forward and to the right of the VC supply column. The marines could see VC starting to scurry in every direction. There was no cover, just open terrain in all directions, with little crevices where one hill stopped and another hill started. Before Goodwin could make corrections Holiday yelled into the radio, "Adjust fire 50 to the left, 10 rounds HE fire for effect, football field pattern". Goodwin, looked at Holiday and said," That's what I was gonna say," and smiled. Holiday grinned back.

The VC were no more than 150-200 yards down the hill from them. They had waited until there were at least 25 VC in sight before calling in the fire mission. The gooks had no idea where the mortars were being directed from, nor, initially, where the small arms fire was either. The marines had lined up, on their bellies on top of their hill and all were shooting at whatever they could see running, through all the smoke, and dust. It was like a turkey shoot. In the middle of it all, Holidays stands up and screams "That's it you sons of bitches! I'll kill you all!". Then screams into the handset, "10 more rounds H E same pattern" Goodwin stares up at him.

"Get down" Simms yells at him. "What are you nuts?"

The VC had scattered and there were none to be seen. Holiday counted 17 dead on the hill, but the rest had vanished into the hills. Holiday was panting hard, still pumping adrenalin, still filled with hate and pain at remembering how his buddy Charlie had died. This was his revenge. Goodwin saw the wild look in his eye, saw his clenched fists by his side, and saw the twisted look of hate on his face.

"Good job, are you ok?"

"Never felt better" Holiday snapped.

> 23 Sept: 67 Killed a sniper today with one mortar round. It was a shot in a million. I am so proud of our gunners. That damn sniper had been following us all day. We got him.

The patrol was squad size. It was just a routine patrol. The grunts went through familiar villages, checking for new faces, checking for IDs, searching for weapons caches or anything out of the ordinary.

Cpl Larimore decided to take the patrol closer to the foothills and away from the river. There were no vils that far from the river, just rice paddies. But it was some place Holiday had never been before. This ought to be interesting. It was.

The patrol cleared the last vile. Ahead were a series of tree lines with one or two hooches, clustered together, but the clusters were scattered over a large area. Looking at his map, Holiday noticed that there were more hooches than he expected. No cluster was big enough to be a vil. Holiday surmised these clusters were of families rather than vils. These families probably had claim to several acres of rice and lived close enough to tend to them regularly.

The patrol started out into the nearest paddy from the vil when a shot rang out. Damn! A sniper, but where was he? It sounded like he was ahead of them and to the right. There was a stand of trees there and a couple of hooches. The grunts advanced in a jog seeking cover among the trees.

Each time the patrol advanced, a shot would ring out. No one could pin point exactly where they were coming from. It seemed for every shot, the direction would change. This went on for a couple of hours.

Larimore spread out the patrol and started advancing towards another set of hooches, looking for the sniper. BLAM! A shot rings out. One Marine down. Shit! Where the hell was he? Holiday ran up to the wounded marine. As the FO radioman, he also doubled as the man who called in medevacs whenever needed. Larimore was already there, scanning the area trying to pinpoint where that sniper could be.

As Holiday called in the medevac, he noticed the entry wound was on the upper right shoulder of the grunt and the exit wound was on the lower left chest. Laramore kept searching the area with his eyes. Not knowing where the sniper was left everyone vulnerable and exposed. He was in deep discussion with a couple of other grunts, trying to decide where to look for the sniper and minimize the risk in doing so.

"Larimore", Holiday whispered. "Look at the angle of the wound. That bastard is in a tree and judging from the angle I'd say no more than 100 yards away and up at least 40 feet." Larimore quickly scanned the area that would fit that bullets trajectory. "There!" Larimore pointed. "One of those 4 trees near that one hooch" He added. "But which one"? Holiday said, "Let me call in a fire mission and just blow the hell out of all those trees". Holiday saw a slow grin form on Larimore's face.

"Yeah; do it".

Holiday took his time calling in the particulars of the fire mission. He had Mueller on the horn and they were comparing maps. Holiday explained to Mueller the exact hooch he wanted to target. When Mueller confirmed he knew which hooch Holiday was referring to, Holiday told him, "There are 4 trees just a quarter inch away from that hooch at 7 o'clock on your map".

"Can you plot one round HE as a marker from the info I gave you, "asked Holiday?

The idea was to use the HE round in lieu of a white phosphorous one, hoping to do some damage with it then adjust fire concentrating 4 rounds in a tight area around those trees.

"One round hotel echo coming right up" replied Mueller. "Do you want cheese with that? "he added. Holiday snorted and said, "You may fire when ready, Gridley". Within seconds there was a loud explosion right at the base of the closest tree. Through all the smoke and dust the mortar kicked up, Larimore and Holiday saw a body fly out of the tree. "Holy shit! Did you see that?" hollered Larimore. Holiday grinned and waving one finger in the air, shouted "ONE round! We got him with one round!" "My guys are good!"

The patrol headed for the body, carefully looking for other snipers. As they approached, Holiday saw that the sniper was a teen aged boy and he was dead. His elation was mixed with sorrow that this young boy, about 15, was now dead. But, he told himself, thus is the nature of war, kill or be killed.

Within a few minutes the medevac chopper showed up and the wounded marine was transported onto the CH-34. Doc had told the patrol that he had a good chance of surviving. For battle hardened marines, this was a good day. One marine would survive and one enemy was dead.

> 3 Oct:67 Monsoons coming soon. Getting cooler at night. Am getting sick of all these night patrols. I have been keeping tabs: for every 3 patrols I go out on, at least one marine gets wounded or killed, mostly by booby traps and snipers. Nasty little war this is. I keep waiting for my turn. When will I get it? Or was my injury from that grenade enough to satisfy the gods of war?

It was a bigger night patrol than usual. Most patrols were no more than a fire team or a squad. But tonight, it was a platoon. Holiday was wondering why. Why the beefed up patrols? Was it because the monsoons were coming and HQ wanted to step up operations before the weather curtailed patrols? Was it because it was during monsoons that Charlie did more supplying from the north and less engagement with the Americans? Was it because the marines had been effective disrupting their supplies and the VC were massing bigger units to fight them with?

Holiday was still pondering these and other questions, when the word came for the platoon to set up an L shaped ambush. Holiday, moved towards the side of the road, and dropped off the side, to position himself on the berm of the road, which was not much wider than a trail. He and Goodwin's job was to ready fire missions in any direction from the point of ambush.

The VC were unpredictable. They could run away

from them through the rice paddies, retrace where they had just come from back down the trail, or try to run through them, to escape the ambush.

Holiday never knew beforehand exactly where the ambush would be staged. The FO team knew the general area where the patrol would go and would work out possible scenarios with the FDC team back on the hill, even before starting out on patrol.

Goodwin and Holiday were whispering to each other setting up coordinates, after finding where they were on the map. Goodwin had placed the map under his poncho and with a red lens flashlight was showing Holiday when the word came down to be quiet. Usually in these type of ambushes the marines would be hiding for hours before any action if there were action at all. But this time, they had not been in the ambush for more than 20 minutes, when the word came.

L shaped ambushes were just that; shaped like an L. The long stem was set up along the trail with riflemen, while the short stem was set up to cross the trail and had at least one machine gun team. With this configuration, any enemy stumbling into this type of ambush would be caught in a deadly crossfire. Sometimes the marines would lineup yards from the trail, and other times they would line up right off the trail, like on the berm of the road, like they were this night. The distance insured more safety for the unit, but cut down on the effectiveness of the ambush. Being on the trail ensured a more effective and deadly ambush, but put the marines at higher risk.

This night, in the pitch black dark and rain and mud, the captain had figured that the enemy would never be able to see them. He was correct on that assumption. Vietnam in the monsoons on overcast and moonless nights was like being in a cave 100 feet underground. It was so dark that one could not see ones hand 3 inches from ones face. But as one could sense a hand in ones face, one could sense when one was not alone in the jungle. It also helped that sounds travel great distances in the jungle, as the quiet marines were witnessing at this very moment.

Holiday could hear the rustle of clothes, and the padding of feet in the mud, from far off down the trail, at least 50 yards. The jungle was deathly quiet on nights like this.

Holiday's heart began to pound within his chest. His breath became short almost gasping breaths. The fear of anticipation on what was about to happen played havoc on his physiology. He was afraid that the noise of his breathing would travel down the trail to the ears of the enemy. Holiday did not want to be the one to tip off the VC that they were there………waiting…for the sole purpose of killing them. Taking lives…brutally.

Holiday did not want to think of it that way, but as destroying the enemy, the killer of his buddies. Although there were times, in the quiet and solitude of his hooch where he often pondered what death was, if life had any purpose, how could human beings be so quick to take another life were they not so far removed from being animals? How one could be alive one instant and dead the next? And he, Mike Holiday had taken lives, several times over, where he knew the dead man was dead because of his expertise and effectiveness. Alive one minute, dead the next.

Holiday's heart was still pounding and he pushed himself further into the mud as he heard the noises coming down the trail, closer.....closer. He tried to regulate his breathing which had started to come in gasps, his chest heaving, so filled with fear was he...he must calm down. He was sure the gooks would hear his breathing. His heart was pounding so hard it was lifting his chest from the mud, and then he heard it. BRRRRRRRRIP! Some asshole had let out a loud fart. All the marines started to snicker and chuckle. Through this noise Holiday could hear the whispers of the VC and the scurrying of feet and the movement of gear, going AWAY from them. The VC had heard the fart and the marines stifling laughs and decided rather than engage their enemy, that discretion was the better part of valor and had run away in the dark.

The marines were still laughing that nervous laughter when Holiday heard the gunny whisper loudly "Who shit?" This prompted another round of snickers and chuckles. "Tain't funny you morons," the gunny continued, "You dumb fucks just fucked up a decent ambush." Holiday could not help but laugh in his poncho, not wanting the gunny to hear him. He felt like a balloon had been pricked and all the fear and tension had been let go. He turned to the marine lying next to and not even seeing his face whispered, "Those gooks are going to go home to their wives and say 'Honey, my life was saved by an American fart'". The faceless marine let out a guffaw. "I'm gonna jam my size 11 boot up the ass of the next idiot that laughs" Holiday heard the gunny spit.

After a brief conference of the LT and gunny, the order was given to head back to the hill. LT knew they would not be able to set up any more ambushes this night. Those VC would spread the word that the marines were there. And those bastards were even better at setting up their own ambushes than the marines were.

> 27 OCt:67 The days are getting colder and wetter. Goodwin got wounded and shipped out. His replacement lasted one week before he got dinged. No other "volunteers" for the job of FO and Sarge didn't want to put a newbie into the position. The gun crews were not up to full compliment. Reinforcements were slow in coming. Sarge asks me if I will be my own FO team. 3 FO's in 9 months and I am still out here in the bush. The shit hit the fan last night.

Holiday was getting sick of all the night patrols in the rain and then after maybe 4 hours sleep, having to go out on day patrols as well. He glanced at his watch 2240. This had been another full platoon patrol, instead of the squad or fire team patrols, he had gotten used to. The platoon was walking the "highway" back to the hill, in staggered column as usual. This patrol had been off the hill since 0600 that morning. Holiday was sure they had walked 40 miles that day. No ambushes had been set up; no fire fights, just moving from vil to vil in their patrol area. It had rained all day and despite the poncho, Holiday had gotten soaked. Most of the guy had taken off their ponchos to give their uniforms a chance to dry.

It had stopped raining about 3 hours ago, although the sky was overcast and the air was heavy and the darkness was all encompassing. Holiday hated those nights when it was so dark you could barely see the man in front of you. You walked along following the sounds rather than actually seeing the man. The darkness made the marine's spacing closer than usual. It was not uncommon when the order came to halt for one marine to walk into the man ahead of him in column.

Holiday was glad when the order came to head back to the hill. He was tired as were all the Marines. They were making good time, not stopping for much and they stayed on the dirt road, which was unusual. Patrols almost always stayed off trails and roads. There were a few reasons for this. To avoid booby traps, and to not give away where they were or what direction their patrol was headed. Holiday could not count the number of times that they walked into the rice paddies rather than stay on the dikes to avoid booby traps. The local farmers hated them for this since this tore up their rice crops.

The LT was making a beeline back to the hill. Holiday wondered if the PFs (popular forces, similar to a militia) had been notified they were coming. There was a PF detachment in the vil immediately to the East of Hill 52. These bozos were ill trained and ill equipped. He did not want allies shooting up the Marines by accident. Holiday wondered why the PFs had been assigned to the vil in the first place. His company had done a marvelous job pacifying the entire area. Most of the villages seemed to like the presence of the Marines. Holiday knew his 81's had been effective in the firefights. The patrols had not run into too much resistance once the monsoons had come. Ever since that operation held on the other side of the river in August, things had seemed to quiet down.

They were nearing the edge of the vil now. Had it not been so damn dark, he would have been able to see the profile of the hill rising up from the paddies, but not tonight. No stars, no moon, not even candles lit in the hutches of the villagers. Well it was late and probably all of them were sleeping, even the PFs, Holiday thought to himself wryly.

RATATATATATAT! It was a roar of small arms fire.

Holiday immediately fell to his knees, pistol drawn, heart pounding. They were everywhere! Through the flashes of muzzles and grenades, Holiday could see dozens of VC. In an instant, Holiday could see the marine in front of him get shot between his trigger finger and middle finger, by the VC not more than 3 feet in front of him. With .45 stretched straight out in front of him, Holiday put 7 rounds into the VC's head. The first round did the job, but he was so scared that he kept firing until he had no more bullets to fire. Fingers fumbling, Holiday reached down on his belt to pull out another clip of ammo and in less than 5 seconds had his .45 loaded cocked and ready. In all the chaos, Holiday would fire at anything that moved. He knew through training and experience that no marine would be up and running around. Only gooks were. But 2 clips do not last long for a .45 and soon enough he was empty. He looked over to the wounded Marine to see if he could use his weapon, but he saw him using his middle finger to pull the trigger, the index finger just dangling.

"BEHIND YOU" shouted the wounded Marine. Holiday quickly turned and saw a gook nearly on top of him with an sks rifle, bayonet extended aimed at his throat. Holiday threw his now empty. 45 at the enemy hitting him in the head, giving him enough time to reach up and grab the weapon, trying to wrench it out of his hands. The VC did not let go, but had fallen down still clutching the rifle as Holiday, crawled up on his body, one hand still grabbing the rifle and the other hand balled up in a fist, smashing blows into the gook's face. "I *can't just beat him up*", Holiday thought to himself, "I *have to kill him*". In one swift move, he smashed his enemy's nose and with the ball of his hand and with all the force he could muster, shoved the nose into the VC's brain. The man immediately went limp. "Hey*! It works*" Holiday thought.

Holiday had trained himself to put his emotions on hold during fire fights. He did not want to do what that arty radioman had done, panic to the point of not being able to function. But this! This hand to hand … his guts were turning over and over.

Holiday grabbed the sks, hoping it was still loaded, tried to fire at other VC still running amuck between and around the marines. Damn! Empty. He looked on the body for clips or rounds, but sensing someone very close by looked up in time to see a VC running by him. He swung out the rifle and smashing it into the gooks legs, caused his to stumble and fall. Holiday scrambled over to his enemy and straddling the body, reached down and with his right hand jammed his thumb on one side of the throat, and with fingers on the other side, squeezed as hard as he could and then twisted and pulled. He felt the trachea collapse. One strike of the butt of the sks on this man's head, and he was still. "*Holy shit*" Holiday thought, "*This works too*"

"81's! 81's" "Holiday get your ass up here!" Holiday heard S/Sgt Prizeman screaming for him. Half running, half crawling, Holiday reached Prizeman. "Call some goddamn illumination rounds over our position NOW!" "Sarge, over the rice paddies, over the river, where?" "Over us you idiot" Prizeman snapped. "Sarge, we get lit up as well as them. These gooks will break either towards the river or the paddies, if you illuminate the river, they will head towards the paddies then we got them" "Holiday, you fucking idiot, I gave you an order, call in illumination right over us, now DO IT". Holiday could see the fear, near panic on Prizeman's face and he could hear it in his voice. This was a lifer. A man who had spent nearly 20 years in the Corps, a prick whom the Grunts hated because he always talked down to them and gave them Mickey Mouse orders...so afraid that he was near hysterical, giving him a stupid order. Where the hell was the LT anyway? He should be giving the order, not Prizeman. "Aye aye Sarge" Holiday sneered. Turning onto his side, Holiday, grabbed his handset and called "Whisky Lima, this is Lima Forward, fire mission 3 round illumination on the red line, on the red line Fire when ready"

Holiday heard the FDC radioman, a funewgy, call back, " Lima Forward, this is Whisky Lima, we need some coordinates" Holiday keyed back and shouted, "At the bottom of the hill you fucking moron, can't you hear all the fire? Get FDC to look it up on the map. I am a bit too fucking busy right now". Holiday heard Sgt Mueller (thank god he got that funewgy off the radio) Roger Lima Forward; 3 rounds Illumination on the red line". Within 20 seconds, the illumination popped overhead.

The darkness was chased away by the brilliance of the 3 rounds, making the battlefield look like high noon. Everyone was lit up. Everyone was exposed. Holiday saw a VC with a burp gun run by Ramos, his buddy, and with a short burst, run a line of bullets from his legs through his chest and into his head. Ramos crumpled like a rag doll. This took a second, but to Holiday, it seemed like 5 minutes. It was as if he saw with clarity every bullet hit Ramos, saw blood squirt out of his thigh, his chest and saw a part of Ramos's head fly off from the force of the bullet hitting his skull.

Holiday still lying on his side, turned to Prizeman and with a twisted face full of rage, screamed, YOU did this you fucking asshole. I told you not to call in Illumination right over us!" "Don't you call me an asshole. I'll have your stripes". Holiday lunged at Prizeman. A marine jumped on his back and knocking him to the flat on the ground whispered loudly in his ear, "Not now. Later. Get him later". Holiday broke down sobbing. Another buddy dies because of the stupidity of a power drunk American.

The fire fight raged all around him as he lay there, face

in the mud, wiping away tears for his dead buddy. Soon enough, another platoon came down from the hill to rescue them. The VC broke it off and ran off into the darkness. Holiday was helped to his feet. The fire fight was over. Three marines lay dead, several wounded including the LT. Holiday went over to Ramos's body, taking his poncho, he placed it on the ground, and gently rolled the body of his friend onto the poncho. Still kneeling, Holiday heard a few marines come over, and gripping the corners of the poncho, helped Holiday lift up the body to carry it up the hill.

Holiday , no pistol, poncho filling up with the blood of his friend, thought how light Ramos felt being carried through the barbed wire gate leading into the compound. As he and the other 3 Marines cleared the gate, Holiday saw several of the 81 gun crew standing about, watching the platoon carry its dead and wounded into the secure area. Still carrying the body of his fallen comrade, Holiday shouted over to one of the gunners, "Smythe, throw me your .45". Without hesitation, Smythe did just that. Holiday caught it in midair and holstered it.

After a few more yards, Holiday placed the body down, and drawing his pistol, walked over to the Captain, who was getting a report from one of the squad leaders, not the LT who was wounded bad, nor from Prizeman, who was second in command of that patrol.

Holding the pistol to his side, Holiday asked the Captain, "Where's Prizeman"? "Secure that weapon, Holiday", the Captain responded. "Where's Prizeman," Holiday shouted back. The squad leader was hurriedly whispering into the Captains ear, the same marine who had forced him to the ground and told him to wait to get his revenge.

"Why do you want to know?" asked the Skipper. "I am going to shoot him, sir," Holiday responded brandishing his borrowed .45. Turning on his heel, Holiday walked off shouting "Prizeman! Prizeman! Where are you?" The squad leader ran up to him to walk with him, guiding him to hooches to look into, took him to the mess tent, the CP tent, the gun pits, seemingly helping him to look for Prizeman.

"You won't find him in the dark", the squad leader nearly whispered. "Let's wait until it gets light and I'll help you look for him". Holiday sunk to his knees and burying his head began sobbing uncontrollably. Sgt Mueller sat in the mud next to him. Placing his hand on Holidays shoulder, said "Tough night, Marine. Get it all out."

The next thing Holiday remembered was waking up in his hooch about mid-day. No one had disturbed him, no one had called him for patrols or to do any duty. They had let him sleep.

8 Oct:67: Ramos is dead. 2 others dead. LT wounded bad. S/Sgt Prizeman is to blame for Ramos's death. I hate these lifers. Just because most of us are in our teens, they think we are just out of boot camp. They talk down to us and they always talk about the Old Corps. Fuck the Old Corps. We bleed red, just like they do. Us young guys know more about how to fight in the bush than any of them, except maybe the gunny. He isn't a lifer. He is a career Marine. All the guys like the gunny. He has balls and he never asks us to do anything he won't do himself.

Holiday knew he had the only CS (tear gas) grenade on the hill. This is not common ordinance for a grunt company. He can't remember how he came across the grenade, but he knew what he was going to do with it. Third platoon, Prizeman's platoon, had agreed to look the other way, were he to throw the grenade into Prizeman's hooch, and then shoot him as he came out to get away from the gas. Make it look like a sniper did it. He planned to do it right at dusk. Dark enough for no one to notice him, but light enough to have it look like a VC like 7 0'clock Charlie did it.

Holiday had arranged with third platoon, for the first night, after the ambush, to throw the gas grenade into Prizeman's hooch. He was walking up the hill from having gone down to buy a coke from the local merchant when he spied the skipper standing by the entrance to the compound. He was tossing a grenade up and down in his hand, like a pitcher would a baseball.

"Is this yours, Holiday?" asked the Captain. "Why would you think that particular grenade would be mine sir? "asked Holiday innocently.

"Because we found it in your hooch and there are no other CS grenades on the hill," Skipper replied. "What were you going to do with this?" the Skipper asked, still tossing the grenade.

" I was going to booby trap the trash pit, sir" Holiday responded thinking fast, " You know how the kids rummage through there looking for food, but taking the old cans to be used as booby traps, so, I was going to set up the CS grenade, to kind of…scare them, sir, didn't want to kill any of them…………Sir"

Captain Pratt stopped tossing the grenade. A smile slowly crept up on his face. "Uh huh" he finally said. "Well marine, you know you should have gotten authorization first, before setting this up"

"I was going to do that today" Holiday interrupted. "I see", said the Captain. "By the way, Marine, S/Sgt Prizeman is no longer part of this company. He is being transferred out at 1300 today by chopper. I do NOT want you anywhere near, the LZ understood?"

"You can thank me anytime, Marine for not having you arrested last night when you threatened to shoot Prizeman. I know what happened and I know why you are upset. This is war and mistakes are made. But I want your word as a United States Marine that should you come upon S/Sgt Prizeman ever again whether it be here or back in the states, you will NOT do anything to him, not even throw a gas grenade at his hooch........." Skipper smiled. "Do I have your word?"

Holiday looked at him for a long minute. He knew the Captain was right. He knew he could not allow his emotions to control him where he would do something stupid. And he knew other men besides Prizeman had made mistakes that had cost lives. But this asshole, was so arrogant, so convinced because he had more stripes he knew better..............."Yes, sir, I understand completely and you have my word." Skipper tossed the grenade back to Holiday.

"That booby trap idea in the trash pit was a good idea. See to it, Marine" the Skipper said. Then he strolled back up to his CP as Holiday, watched him go. "Aye aye, Sir" Holiday muttered to himself.

> 21 Oct:67 Woke up and saw everything under water for as far as the eye can see. The only thing I could see were the tops of the trees. I can't see any hooches, not even the roofs. I wonder where all the people went? I wonder if it is like this all the way to the sea. This is unbelievable. One good thing, no patrols for awhile , unless they put us in rowboats. Got a new man today. He is a shitbird, cocky, stupid and a loud mouth.

Holiday had gotten more sullen, since the death of Ramos. Funewgies coming over from the states were talking about people protesting the war, kids his own age, in the streets, throwing bombs, Molotov cocktails; hell if they wanted violence they could come here. At least it would be against the enemy and not their own citizens. What don't they understand about why we are here? S Vietnam was a member of SEATO and had asked for our help. The N Vietnamese had attacked one of our gun boats. They were commies and they were trying to take over the world, just like Hitler before.

Holiday remembered in school one day, looking at a world map. All countries colored green were considered democracies, those pink were socialist and those red were communist. He saw very little green; lots of red and pink. It scared him. Blue were nonaligned dictatorships or oligarchies. Lots of blue in the Middle East, ironic, blue being the color of water, in desert countries.

Why can't those kids see this part of the cold war was hot and their fellow countrymen were dying, trying to save a backward country from takeover by Communists.

Holiday was still pondering the purpose of being in Nam when his poncho was pulled back from the hatchway of the hooch. "Sarge wants you". Holiday looked up at the soaking wet gyrene. He liked Sgt Mueller far more than that lifer SOB before him, but wondered why Sarge wanted him. He could not go on patrols, not with everything flooded and he knew Sarge would not put him on shitter detail. "Be right there," Holiday replied.

Holiday fumbled for the other poncho, and slipping it on, went out into the non-stop downpour. *"Damn these monsoons"* Holiday thought to himself. Holiday negotiated the 6 steps, made of ammo boxes, to the interior of the FDC hutch. Sgt Mueller was there, with a skinny, baby faced funewgy. "This is Corporal Hawks, Sgt told Holiday. *"Shit*, Holiday thought to himself, *"a funewgy is E-4 and I am still E-3."*

"How long in country" asked Holiday, eying up the funewgy. "A week" was the reply. "Well, listen up," Holiday continued. "This isn't ITR (infantry training regiment) anymore. These gooks are trying to kill you."

"There ain't no gook good enough to kill my ass," Hawks interrupted. Mueller watched the disgust enter into Holidays eyes. He had seen it before as new guys; try to put up a false bravado. Mueller, shook his head, and said to Hawks, "Son, listen to Holiday, he can teach you how to survive." Hawks, retorted "No disrespect to your rank Sarge, but I ain't your son". Holiday watched the disgust enter into Mueller's eyes. *This Billy bootband is not going to last a week*

28 Oct:67 Had to save a funewgy's ass today. The marines must be scraping the bottom of the barrel. I do not like the asshole. He is going to get someone killed if he doesn't get killed first. Next time he doesn't duck I am not going to risk my ass to save his. Been in country

almost 10 months now. It feels like 10 years. There has got to be more to life than killing.

"Saddle up". Holiday heard the order. Jumping into his gear and strapping on his radio, Holiday sauntered outside his hooch, to see the first platoon gathering near the East gate. "Where to today, sir" Holiday asked the LT. Ambush Valley, grinned the Lieutenant. "Holiday, I hear you are bringing out the new radioman with you today. "Yes sir" Holiday answered. "Keep him alive, Holiday. I'd rather have you as FO than back as radioman." Aye aye sir"

Holiday had approached Sgt Mueller a few weeks ago, when his latest FO had been medevacked out after having stepped on a booby trap. Holiday had refused to train anymore. Since Charlie's death, Holiday had trained 3 other FO's. He had made a deal that he would act as FO and radioman, a one man team, rather than see another marine on his team get killed or wounded. Sgt Mueller had agreed. He had felt the same anxiety and the same pain seeing men under his command get hit. Holiday had survived 4 F.O.s. He knew this had taken a toll on Holiday, who he had seen withdraw from the other men, stay to himself and ignore the comradery the others seem to enjoy. His 2 gun crews were a tight bunch. They all pitched in when a new guy came to replace someone shipping out. The only casualties Mueller had seen under his command were the F.O.s.

His gun crews seem to leave Holiday alone as if hanging out with him would spell their doom. Holiday must have felt like the most unlucky man in the outfit, seeing 4 men on his team die or get wounded. It's as if he ignored the fact that in the 81's group, he and his FO were the only ones facing the enemy daily with the constant patrols he was put on. The company used Holiday a lot, since he was their "artillery" when they got into firefights. They even used him on 4 man fire teams, setting up observation posts on high ground searching for gooks on the Ho Chi Min trail. As a result, Mueller let Holiday sleep during the day and hardly ever put him on work details. This, Mueller believed, also contributed to the distance Holiday had put between himself and the rest of the outfit. In fact, when Holiday did "socialize" which was rare, it was usually with the grunts. The regular infantry, the ones he spent all his time with on patrols.

So, Mueller, rather than chance another man as FO, had allowed Holiday to act as his own FO and radioman. He did manage, however to get a new FDC radioman, but had planned on Hawks learning the FO radioman position and using Holiday as FDC radioman, only he hadn't told Holiday any of this yet. As far as Holiday new, he was training Hawks to be HIS radioman while he took on the role of FO.

Holiday eyed Hawks, and checked to see if he had all his gear. "Move out" LT ordered, and the platoon began walking down the side of the hill in single file. "Behind me Hawks", Holiday told the funewgy. "Well yes SIR Lance Corporal," Hawks snapped.

Holiday felt his blood begin to rise. "Listen Cpl funewgy," Holiday snapped back, "the radioman always walks behind the FO. When I need the radio, you come to me since I am the one calling in the fire mission , not the FO going to you. Got that Cpl asshole?"

Hawks muttered something under his breath, which Holiday did not hear nor care to hear. His hearing had been damaged in a mortar attack a few months ago. He had told no one not wanting to use his hearing loss as an excuse to get out of the field. He knew if they did take him out, he would not be used as a radioman, nor cross trained for any other MOS, but be used for every shit detail back in battalion. Holiday would rather take his chances in the bush and feel like he was doing something useful than be safe as part of the "in the rear with the gear gang" burning shitters and putting up concertina daily, or digging trenches.

For a week after the mortar attack, Holiday would be sitting or walking patrol and just fall over. He always had said he lost his footing. His eardrum had been damaged. His platoon had intended on sweeping a vil just ahead of them. They had about 100 yards in the rice paddy to cover when the gooks opened up with a mortar attack. In a mortar attack when in open terrain, the marines had been taught to run towards the mortars. This forced the enemy gunners to keep cranking their guns up bringing the fire closer to their own position, There was a bank of soft dirt just ahead, wet dirt that he and a few others had jumped behind when the mortars had started to fall.

He had pushed his face as far into the mud as he could with his face turned to the left and having his mouth opened as he had been trained to do, to try and equalize the pressure from the concussions of the exploding mortars. One or two had landed so close to where he had been lying that the ground shook and mud and debris had rained all around him.

Mortars, unlike artillery shells exploded in a cone configuration, rather than more like a pancake as the 105's or 155 artillery shells were prone to do. When the barrage had ended, the man next to him had peaked up from behind the mound of mud they both had been behind, when the last mortar exploded not more than 20 feet from their position. Holiday watched the man's head snap back, and even over the sound of the explosion, had heard his neck break. He watched in horror as the body slumped to the ground with the man's head screwed in an unnatural position. He knew the man was dead. The lifeless eyes were boring into the air, mouth open in a death gape. Holiday had not even heard a death rattle. But he knew Henderson was dead. This same mortar was the one that blown out his eardrum. The ensuing temporary deafness had added to the eeriness of Henderson's lifeless expression and the deafening silence that followed.

Holiday had heard his own muffled cry for the corpsman, watched the doc run over and ask him who was hit. Holiday had pointed to Henderson and had said, that his neck was broke, barley hearing himself shout this to doc. Holiday had handed his handset to another marine who was now there telling him to call in a medevac. Everyone had assumed he was too much in shock to do it himself, but the truth was he could not hear, but told no one.

It took about the rest of the day for the ringing to go away, but while continuing the patrol, Holiday had felt himself stagger to one side repeatedly, nearly falling down on several occasions. Since the ground was wet, it was here that Holiday used the excuse of slipping in the mud for each time he would fall over: losing his balance from the damage done to his ear.

By the time Hawks had become part of the unit, Holiday had taught himself to watch men's mouths as they talked to mask his inability to actually hear the sounds made to form words. Without doing this, all he heard was someone talking like they had their hand over their mouth. Holiday was secretly proud of himself for keeping his injury a secret. He'd be dammed before he'd wind up burning shitters.

Before long Holiday noticed that the platoon had made it to the mouth of Ambush Valley without incident. He stayed with the CP group as second squad snuck further into the valley, to stage their pretend firefight. The hope was that the enemy would come down to investigate. The LT had even thought to bring a US Carbine which seemed to be the weapon of choice for the VC. These were weapons HO Chi Min had been able to procure from the US during WWII to fight the Japs. They had a distinctive sound, a sharper "crack" when fired.

Sitting in the mud, Holiday said nothing to Hawks, who had been trying to engage him in small talk, mostly complaining about how bored he was. He could hear the pretend fire fight further up the valley. He was listening to see how realistic it would sound, timing being everything. That is, to time the weapons firing as if it were indeed a realistic fire fight. After a few moments, Holiday grunted his approval. "*Yeah. It sounded real enough*", he thought to himself.

Second squad was to stay where they were, and set up their own ambush hoping to have drawn down the VC to come and investigate. Lt was now going to make a big show out of his troops leaving, so the VC could see where the gyrenes were, and hopefully they would assume they were all leaving, including second squad.

He was barking orders….loudly and in plain view of

any VC observing us from the Valley ridges. "Saddle up, first squad take point," he was shouting. As the platoon, minus second squad started to form up for the return to the hill, a 30 caliber machine gun suddenly opened up. Every marine hit the deck, except one; the funewgy, Hawks. "Is that our guys doing another fake ambush?" he inquired. Holiday, already on the deck was watching the 30 caliber bullets hitting the rice paddies in a long sweep from right to left.

"Get down, you stupid asshole," Holiday screamed as he sprang up and tackled Hawks.

Just as he did, the sweep of the machine gun's bullets shot through where Hawks had been standing. *"I should have let him get shot",* Holiday thought to himself.

3 November:67 If I ever see that bastard Hawks in the world I am going to kick his ass …again. He almost got me killed last night. What a shitbird. Where did the Marines dig up this asshole? Makes me wonder, don't we have enough men to replace the ones lost? How many have we lost? Since keeping this log I have figured out that for every third time we go on patrol or set up an ambush, someone either gets hurt or killed: ,mostly by booby traps, some by snipers, a few in fire fights. Snipers are the scariest, especially if one stalks you. If you are careful, and look where you step, you can get lucky and avoid booby traps. Firefights are not scary until after it's over. Too damn busy to be scared when its happening. But sometimes, afterwards, I get the shakes and my stomach turns a lot. I break out in sweats and

have trouble breathing My heart keeps jumping I try to
put it out of my mind, but its hard to do.

Sgt Mueller had decided to let Holiday stay back from
patrols and let Hawks do FO radio while he would do
FDC radio. But that was on condition that he train the
latest piece of cannon fodder to be sent from the states
to become FO; a Cpl Bruner. Mueller had reasoned that
Holiday had seen enough combat, had done double duty
as FO and FO radioman and it was time for a funewgy
to take over, and for Holiday to have his chances of
survival increased.

The 81 CP hooch was dug into the ground about 4
feet, with another 3 feet of piled sandbags making the
hooch's walls above ground. The overhead was planked
with 2x6's, then 3 layers of sandbags were piled on top
of that. The width of this hooch was about 9 feet and
the length was 15 feet. Hinged ammo boxes had been
built into the bulkheads to act as portals, when the lids
could be opened or closed depending on the weather
or if there was an attack.

A few months previous, the company had "procured" a
generator that was situated further up the hill, next to
the chow hall, but this hooch, since it was considered
a command post had been given an electrical line from
the generator. Two light bulbs had been strung from
the 7foot high overhead. It cast enough light for what
Holiday was doing with the funewgy, Bruner.

The aft bulkhead had bunk beds or "racks" as they were called by Marines. The port side had a long bench, that the marines had built from scrap wood and it was on this bench that Holiday sat with Bruner, teaching him how to set up night defensive fire, when on night ambush or night patrol.

The forward bulkhead had the 81 plotting board also made of scrap plywood and 2x4's, plus the radio. To the right of this was the passageway, leading up and out, the steps were constructed of discarded ammo boxes, dug into the dirt. For a sandbag bunker, it was quite cozy.

Sgt Mueller was leaning against the plotting board. 2 other marines were sitting on the racks, talking sports, women, sex and "home". Holiday was sitting with Bruner on the makeshift bench. Holiday had a 2x2 piece of plywood on his lap, with a map pinned to it, using it to show Bruner how to set up fire missions.

"Well, I am going to the holes." Holiday looks up to see Hawks, standing by the hatch, tossing a grenade up and down with one hand. *IDIOT*, Holiday thought to himself. Then out loud he says to Hawks, "Quit tossing that grenade around dimwit" "The pin is in it", retorts Hawks. Holiday, gets a flash of seeing that marine blow himself up when the pin somehow got knocked out of a LAW he had just thrown over his shoulder, when he first arrived country" Mueller sees the flash of anger in

Holidays eyes and says calmly but firmly, to Hawks, " Secure that grenade and go onto your hole."

The "hole" was a sandbagged structure, halfway dug into the ground like this CP hutch, where marines stood or sat, while on guard duty. There were several of these dug in all around the hill. Sgt Mueller had never ordered Holiday to do any "hole watch". He had felt that with all the night patrols he had been on, that when he was back on the hill, he needed a good night's sleep. The other reason was, he did not like Hawks any more than Holiday did and put Hawks on "hole watch" as a way to fuck with him.

Holiday looked back down to the map on the board and picked up with where he had left off, with Bruner. Within seconds he heard: "IF I'M GOING YOU"RE GOING TOO MOTHERFUCKER" as a marine was leaning back and away while reaching for his rifle; and at the same time heard Bruner say, "Oh my god I'm dead" as Bruner scrambled half over Holidays lap and half on the deck, towards the aft part of the hutch.

Holiday looked up to see Hawks had disappeared, but the grenade he had been playing with was on the deck, with no pin in it. Instantly, Holiday dove for the grenade using his plotting board as a barrier to try and muffle the damage this grenade would do in such a small enclosed area. He couldn't get the board to push the grenade into the deck, since the deck was also made out of planks, with the board careening wildly from one side to the other as he tried to push the board into the grenade. *This ain't gonna work*, Holiday thought to himself. It was then he realized if that grenade exploded it would take his head clean off his shoulders. He abandoned the board, and scrambled as far away from the grenade as the confined space would allow him, and shoved his head under a foot stool hoping this would at least protect him from having his brains blown out. He waited for the grenade to rip up his exposed rear end and back, thinking to himself, *"I might survive this if it just takes off my ass"*

The 4 seconds it takes for a grenade to explode once the pin was pulled, seemed to take forever. The entire episode from hearing Bruner scream, to sticking his head under the stool, took about 3 seconds.......now 4...nothing. Nothing. Hot damn! A dud!

Holiday, gingerly peeked out from under the stool, and slowly approached the grenade. Picking it up gently, he unscrewed the clip from the body of the grenade. NO primer. Just then Hawks scrambles down the ammo box steps and in a loud guffaw, says, "Hey motherfuckers did you like that joke? It's a fucking dud"!

Holiday instantly grabbed Hawks by his throat and with his hand firmly around his neck, began to walk Hawks back up the steps, saying in a half hiss, half sneer, " No one is laughing, you fucking moron" He got Hawks up on level ground and with his hand still around his throat, hauled off and hit him so hard in the face, that he felt Hawks go limp. Holiday released his grip and Hawks slumped to the ground, knocked out. Holiday reached down and grabbing his shirt in a ball of cloth, punched him twice more, before Mueller could scramble up the steps to ask, "Well Holiday, did Hawks fall into the trench and you are pulling him out? "Yeah Sarge, that's what happened, Holiday muttered as he released his grip. Holiday walked off into the night, rage still in his chest from the "joke".

> 4Nov: 67 That shitbird, tried to get me busted. Sgt Miller took care of him. I had to shoot Hector this morning. I won't miss him. I will let the rest of my bunkmates live. There are Gertrude and Beatrice, 2 "fuck-you" lizards, Tom and Dick, 2 queer rats, Hernandez, the 13 inch centipede and Freddy, the one eyed frog. I like Freddy, since I see him as a war casualty, who always pees on my rack.

Holiday woke up with a start. He sensed someone or something staring at him. Looking to his left, he saw Hector, the bamboo viper on the sandbag wall of his hutch, the front part of his body extended in space with his head no more than 2 feet from his face, his tongue flicking the air as his glaring eyes kept staring at Holiday. Holiday slowly reached under his cot, pulling his .45 from its holster, and pulling back the slide, aimed his pistol right at Hector's head, hoping that "two-step" would not strike before he could get a shot off.

BLAM BLAM BLAM! Three quick shots and Hector was gone. My god that snake was fast!

Holiday jumped from his cot and stepping outside, saw Hector struggling to make it to the weeds on the side of the hill. Hector was wounded and in great pain was moving as fast as it could. Holiday got within a foot of the snake, and shot him again, killing him. By this time, a dozen marines were running up to his position, with Gunny yelling, "Who fired those shots"? Gunny stopped and putting his hands on his hips, looked over to Holiday, and in his southern drawl said, " Damn, Marine, it took you 4 shots to kill that thing?" Shaking his head and turning away was heard muttering something about damn Yankees not being able to hit the broad side of a barn.

Holiday went to the FDC bunker to tell Sgt Mueller what had happened. Coming down the steps, he overheard Hawkes, on the radio reporting an "assault and battery" on himself, perpetrated by Holiday. Before Holiday could react, he heard Sgt Mueller coming down the steps. Hawkes held out the handset to Mueller and said, "Battalion wants to talk to you". Mueller ripped the handset out of his hands and pushing Hawkes against the bulkhead, and putting his nose against Hawke's nose, whispered, "You gonna report I just assaulted you"? The next few minutes, Holiday heard Mueller explain that there was no assault; that Hawkes had played a joke, and running up the steps into the darkness, had stumbled into the trench... it being dark and all. Holiday had merely tried to pull Hawkes out of the trench and his hand slipped and Hawkes fell back into the trench, and he, Sgt Mueller had witnessed the entire incident.

Sgt Mueller, almost growling at Hawkes, said, "If you EVER go over my head again, I will bust you down to private and give you every shit detail I can think of. Now get the fuck out of my sight. Hawkes starts to move towards the hatch and Holiday pushes him into the plotting board. Sliding off the board, Hawkes hits the deck hard. Holiday, snorts "Hey Hawkes need a hand up"? Then laughs. Hawkes scurries up the steps and out of sight.

> 8 Nov:67 Took a female POW into regiment and then went on to Danang. It was good to get off the hill for a few days. Stopped a rape and saw a kid get blown away. This is a nasty little war. Hard to tell who are the good guys and who are the bad guys.

"Holiday", Sgt Mueller called. "The skipper wants you to take a POW into regimental HQ." "Why me?" inquired Holiday. "Cuz you are a short timer sitting on your ass doing nothing," Mueller grinned. "Nah, the skipper said there are no plans over the next couple of days where 81's will be needed on patrols.....anyway, after the other night, you could stand an in country R&R. Stay in Danang an extra day; go to the PX".

Holiday smiled. *This Sarge is an ok guy, not like that lifer we had when I first got over here.*

It was an occurrence to see a 5x5 truck on the hill. The company was so far out from the main traffic routes that the road was no more than a foot path in some places. Never-the-less, it was here. It had dropped off supplies which choppers usually did and was there to pick up the prisoner. A marine had the prisoner under escort and was loading her up in the back of the truck. Holiday climbed up to join the prisoner and marine. He recognized him as a rifleman from first platoon.

The marine grinned at him. "I volunteered for this; just look at her" Holiday looked over at the prisoner. She was his age, maybe a year or two older, but absolutely gorgeous. Long black hair, signifying she was single. Married women put their hair into buns, but single women did not. Holiday looked into her almond eyes. He saw intelligence, and fear mixed with a hint of hate and confusion. She was about 5'4 and not an ounce of fat on her. She was dressed in typical peasant garb, black silk trousers and a white blouse. Holiday could tell there was no bra underneath. She didn't need one. Her breasts were firm and round. She had the most beautiful face he had ever seen on a Vietnamese woman, in a country with literally millions of beautiful women. Holiday took a seat towards the cab while the other marine stationed himself near the gate of the truck. The bench seats were down and the prisoner sat demurely and quietly on the left side.

"Chester is my name," the marine said while nodding at Holiday. Holiday nodded in reply not finding a need to introduce himself. The truck lurched forward and started down the steep hill pausing only briefly at the gate made of barbed wire and concertina. Then off it roared.

Holiday looked over at the POW. She had a typical cone shaped peasant hat made of bamboo on her head, and her hands were tied with a slip of rope. There was a canvas bag on the deck; Holiday surmised it had been used to cover her head while being transported. Apparently she had been carted in here from somewhere else. As is typical of marines No one told him anything about whom she was, why she was picked up, only where he was to take her. *It's not for marines to question why, only for marines to do or die.*

They drove through a few vils down the "red line". Holiday was enjoying the breeze on his face. He noticed that Chester kept ogling the woman. Holiday tried to concentrate on looking for anything suspicious along the road. He was always aware of booby traps and hoped the road had been swept clean and there would be no trouble. Chester had been chattering on telling stories where all the sentences began with the word "I". Holiday kept silent and letting him ramble on, until he heard or thought he heard Chester say "I am going to get me a piece of that. Glancing up he saw Chester grab a breast on the woman and saw her stiffen up. She had been sitting silently almost like a statue throughout the entire trip.

"What do you think you are doing"? Holiday inquired. "Gonna get me some of that," Chester replied as he grabbed at her again, then started rubbing her leg. "I don't think so" Holiday retorted. "Look at her" Chester continued. "Ain't she a fine example of a female? I bet she would be a good fuck" "What you gonna do stop me? Say I can go first and you can have sloppy seconds" "I don't think so" Holiday repeated. "What's the matter with you? She is only a gook" Chester switched his seat so he was sitting next to the terrified woman. Putting his arm around her he began fondling her breast with his other hand.

"Knock it off" Holiday said.

"Or what, you gonna shoot me"?

Holiday had already slipped his .45 out of its holster while Chester had been pre-occupied with the woman. "As a matter of fact, yes", Holiday answered, raising his pistol. :"

"Shit, what are you a faggot?" Chester stared at him with hate building up in his eyes. Holiday responded,

"You shouldn't call a man a faggot when he has a gun pointed at your heart", Holiday smiled.

"She is a woman not a piece of meat and not here for you to get your jollies off."

Leaning forward, .45 still trained on Chester, he continued. "And I am not going to sit by and see you rape that woman, now get your hands off of her." Holiday glared at the man, his finger tensing up on the trigger.

Chester gave him a long, hard look After a moment of both men staring at each other, Chester leaned back, removed his arm and said, " You are one crazy mother fucker" "I just wanted to have me some fun". The woman had sat quietly though out, staring straight ahead, not looking at either man.

An hour later, they were approaching Dai Loc, battalion HQ, and a fair sized town. The woman put her head down on her lap. Chester, still smarting from having a gun pointed at him, angrily grabbed the woman, and standing her up, shouted. "Stand up bitch, let the town see we got ourselves another VC." Holiday immediately stood up, pistol in hand, jammed the barrel in Chester's face and pushing him down with it, snarled, " We don't know what she is, asshole. "YOU sit down, fuckhead" "One more stunt from you and I report you to the captain".

Grabbing the woman, he sat her down and placed the

canvas sack over her head. He thought she might be an informer for all he knew or was just in the wrong place at the wrong time, or maybe she was VC but he was not about to humiliate her in front of the people they were driving by.

When the truck got to the check point at the base of Hill 37, which was battalion, Chester jumped out of the truck. "You take her onto to Regiment, I am done with you ya crazy prick" "I am getting me a hot meal, some dope and taking it easy. See you back on the hill asshole" .Then, flipping off Holiday, turning, he laughed, and started over to the guards at the check point; probably to score some pot. The truck roared off. Holiday heard Chester shout over the din, "Semper fi, you fucking lifer"

The truck proceeded on to Hill 55, regimental HQ without further incident. As soon as they were away from the town of Dai Loc, Holiday removed the sack from the woman's head.

It angered him that, an American, a MARINE, had tried to rape a woman. He had heard and seen atrocities that the VC had done to their own people. He had seen a dead marine floating face down in the river, who had had his penis and scrotum cut off and sewn in his mouth. *Are we no better than they?*

Holiday jumped out of the truck and holding onto the woman's arm, took her towards S-2, the intelligence hooch. He couldn't leave her outside while he reported in so he took her inside the hooch with him. A major immediately jumped up from his seat, and pushing Holiday outside began screaming at him for being a stupid ass bringing a prisoner into S-2. Holiday calmly waited for him to finish, when the major asked, "Did you bring in this prisoner by yourself?" "No sir, but the other guy jumped out at Hill 37. I couldn't leave her alone out here, sir and I had to report in." The major grunted and told him where to take the woman for questioning. Holiday got to the designated spot and waited until an interrogator showed up.

The young interrogator, told the woman, in Vietnamese to sit down. She turned to Holiday with a question in her eyes. Holiday nodded yes. She sat down. The other marine began asking her for ID, her name, what village was she from. Again she looked at Holiday. Holiday nodded. The woman began to answer the questions put to her. The interrogator, realizing what was happening, snapped, "You can go marine. I can take it from here."

"Sure thing", Holiday replied and turned away walking off. He had not gone 5 paces when he felt eyes on the back of his head. Turning around he saw that woman looking at him, pleading, it seemed with her eyes; that and a look of gratitude. The interrogator was busily asking questions, ignoring the communication happening between the woman and the 19 year old, tired marine. Holiday felt funny in his stomach, but realizing there was nothing else he could do, turned and walked hastily way. He would be haunted by that look, the rest of his life.

Sgt Mueller had told him to go onto Danang for some R&R, so Holiday caught the next convoy heading in that direction. By now Holiday had developed an aversion towards anything that hinted of Mickey Mouse, so he decided he would bunk up in Dog Patch. Holiday could not understand why the USMC still insisted on military decorum when back in the rear. His hill had developed a comradery among the troops, which seemed to work far better than strict military protocol.

In the bush the troops didn't bother to salute, however respect was given to those with rank. Holiday realized there were two types of respect: that which one was entitled to by title such as Captain, Sergeant and that which was earned no matter what rank one had. Officers were still called "sir" but there was a different attitude when the captain was called sir than when Lieutenant Krabb was called sir. Holiday understood the need for protocol but the marines seemed to always take it to the extreme. And Holiday saw many who had rank, abuse their authority.

He recalled coming off an all-night patrol and Sgt Mueller saying, "Hey Holiday give us a hand at filling these sand bags" and his willingness to do that hot back breaking work, because Sarge had asked him to. He contrasted that against Sgt Stoltz saying to him, as he joined the gun crews from returning from an all-night patrol, " Holiday there will be a weapons inspection at 1300 today. You WILL be there"

Holiday had immediately gone to his hooch to sleep and woke up just minutes before the inspection. Not bothering to wear a clean uniform, or even scrape the mud off his boots he joined ranks while Stoltz conducted his weapons inspection. His uniform had dried from wading rivers and ponds on the patrol but his leather holster was still damp and crusted with mud. When it came time for him to draw his weapon, rather than do it militarily, he casually unsnapped his holster, pulled out the .45, slid back the slide and "presented" his weapon. Stoltz gingerly took it with two fingers, glaring at Holiday had barked, "What the hell is THIS"? The pistol was caked with mud, and even had a few rust spots.

Holidays reply was to say, in a mock military voice, "SARGE…….well that is a gas operated semi–automatic pistol with a .45 caliber projectile that can't hit the side of a barn, but if it ever did it would blow one hell of a hole in it" and smiled. Stoltz had moved his face close to Holidays and hissed. "I can have you court martialed for presenting an inoperable weapon for inspection."

Holiday had hissed back, "Get out of my face Sarge, this isn't boot camp" .

"Next time you want to play Mickey Mouse, make sure I can make the game." I have been awake for over 26 hours crawling through the mud, fording rivers and chasing gooks all night. I am entitled to some sleep before you throw an inspection at me."

"You are a marine and you will act like one" Stoltz shouted. Holiday sneered, "Do you want to see if this weapon is operable Sarge?" Stoltz was a stupid man but he did understand the veiled threat. "Get out of my sight and clean that weapon" "Sure thing Sarge," Holiday grunted as he broke ranks and headed for the mess tent.

Holiday had no respect for Stoltz, despite his rank. He had not earned it. Holiday recalled the time when the hill got hit. Previous to this, Stoltz had ordered trenches dug from the ammo pit to the gun pits, so in case of such an event ammo could be transported in relative safety. The trenches were 4 feet deep, but narrow. Ammo boxes would have to be carried on one's shoulder to navigate the trenches. But then Sarge in his infinite wisdom had decided to build foot bridges in several spots over the trench…..for safety reasons. I guess he thought the troops would not be clever enough to jump the trench when crossing it.

Years later, this type of mentality was to become

predominate via federal regulations and laws passed by Congress. OSHA would have been proud of Stoltz's foot bridges. Holiday would be reminded of Stoltz's bridges and that incident where a marine almost died due to no one having a license to drive a mule, in later years by an incident that actually happened. It seems workers had been digging a long trench, at a construction site when the walls of the trench caved in on a few of the laborers. Several men jumped in to try and dig them out before they suffocated to death. OSHA, in its infinite wisdom cited the workers for doing so without having their hard hats on and fined the company several thousand dollars. Creeping socialism Holiday called it. People in power had a tendency to think they knew what was best and devised, well meaning, but usually stupid regulations, like this trench with foot bridges.

Anyway, back to the time the hill was hit. The gun crews were in their pits pumping out mortars as fast as the gunner could pop them in the tube and the gun crew could prep the rounds. Holiday had been assigned to hump the ammo from the ammo pit to the gun pits and had been ordered to use the trenches.

Each case held 3 rounds. The cases were longer than the trench was wide so the case had to be shouldered. However when one came to the foot bridge, the case had to be set down, the carrier had to squat underneath the bridge, then reach back drag, the ammo box over and place it again on his shoulder. This had to be done

3 times between the ammo pit and gun pit. It was very time consuming. In Holidays mind it defeated the purpose for the trench, to be able to transport the ammo quickly and safely.

Holiday opted to not use the trenches at all. It was more important to keep the flow of ammo going than to worry about getting hit with any stray round. As he was moving quickly with an ammo box held in front of him, (easier than hoisting on one's shoulders) he heard his name shouted out above the din off all the noises of combat. Holiday stopped, looking around for the source of the shout. Looking down he saw the eyes and forehead of Stoltz hugged close to the wall of the trench. To Holiday it looked like that comical character of Kilroy from the Korean War. Holiday could not help but burst out laughing. Stoltz in his fear probably could not ever fathom why a man exposed to enemy fire while carrying ammo boxes had burst out laughing. "Holiday! Get down in the trench" Holiday shouted back, "Your bridges make that impossible Sarge". Then under his breath, " You dumb fuck".

No. Holiday had no respect for Sergeant Stoltz. Holiday would see this type of mindless adherence to stupid regulations played out over and over in civilian life, by petty people put in positions of authority who would get there by adhering to the regs in lieu of getting the job done. Regulations have a habit of deterring accomplishing the goal.

The most outrageous example of this mindless adherence to regulations happened when Holiday had been in country less than a month. While standing in chow line one afternoon a sniper had shot a marine standing no more than 10 feet in front of him. Every one hit the deck. A couple of marines crawled over to the wounded marine. Another marine had jumped onto a mule (an 8x4 flatbed 4 wheel drive vehicle) Several marines had picked up the marine and carried him over to the mule.

From out of the crowd a staff sergeant had appeared. "Marine," he shouted to the driver, "Are you licensed to drive that vehicle?" "No Sarge, but we need to get that man over to BAS (battalion aid station) "Get off the vehicle" the Sarge replied, then turning to the bunch still waiting for chow asked" Any marines qualified on the mule?" Silence, then….. "I am Sarge" from a voice in the crowd. "Produce your license" barked the staff sergeant. "It's back in my hooch…"then go get it" the Sgt shouted. "NO one drives this vehicle unless properly authorized to do so," he lectured.

Meanwhile, the wounded marine, bleeding profusely was near death. A corpsman came out of nowhere and jumping onto the mule, cranked it up. "Marine, show me your…….." No time Sarge and I am not a marine but a navy corpsman, take it up with my CO at BAS". (Battalion Aid Station) Off he roared with the cheers of the marines echoing in his ear.

Holiday thought to himself *that bastard would see this man die for want of a goddamn license to operate a mule. This is insane.*

Holiday continued on to Danang, hoping to hit the PX before it got dark so he could sneak into Dogpatch at dusk; dark enough to slip in but not so dark as to leave himself vulnerable. Rumor was VC also visited Dogpatch. He better find a buddy to go with him. It was safer to have someone watching your back

Dogpatch was a vil of sorts halfway between the PX and the Airstrip. Anything a man wanted could be gotten there at far less prices than found in the PX. Dogpatch also offered items never found in the PX, including dope, if one indulged and more and more it seemed servicemen WERE indulging; women for the night, cheap, beer, hard liquor, music, but Holiday thought spending the night with someone soft and feminine was what was needed. It was a place to put the war on hold for a night, a place to forget about the death, the fear, the mud, the leeches, the scorpions, a place to relax, drink some beer and hear female laughter. And get a little tail.

> 10 Nov: 67 Saw a kid get blown away today. The PF knew he was a VC. The kid was no more than 10 years old. The PF shot him dead. What kind of people send their kids to die? Do they hate us that much? Or is it that they think life is cheap here. I know this country has been fighting one war or another since even before 1941, with the Japs, then the French , now us and we are

here trying to save their asses. Marine Corps birthday today. Whoopdy fuckin do.

The next morning, Holiday decided he would have breakfast at the base mess hall. He detoured over to a unit of engineers (they always had the best showers) to see a buddy who had gone through staging at Camp Pendleton with him before shipping over. After shooting the breeze with him and taking the best shower he had had since coming to Nam, both he and his buddy sauntered over to the mess hall, for chow.

Standing in line wasn't so bad when you had a buddy with you. He and Roberts, exchanged stories of their activities since they had split up that first night, he being assigned to 7th regiment and Roberts to this engineering unit. As they settled in to chow down, a group of grunts sat in a table next to them. These marines were obvious visitors to Da Nang, probably having gotten a ride from a 5x5 earlier that day. They were dirty, stinky, and needed haircuts and shaves. Holiday looked at their eyes. They all had that look that combat marines get. It was a combination of a dead look with flashes of anger, tiredness, alertness and fear. Holiday KNEW that look.

As he sat there trying to figure out what outfit these guys belonged to, he overheard a Remington raider complain that they had vanilla ice cream, yet again, and that it was melting by the time they got their dish full. Holiday wondered if when they got back to the world, if their war stories would consist of telling their grandkids of the hardships they had to suffer through, having vanilla ice cream again! And melting ice cream at that!

The grunts must have over heard this whiner. Almost on cue, they all started to eat like pigs, literally. They ignored their utensils and ate with their hands, scooping up mashed potatoes with their fingers and shoveling it into their mouths, grabbing their steaks and growling as they bit off chunks, then chewing with their mouths open, grunting at each other, wiping their hands on their utilities, drinking milk until it spilled out of the cups and down their faces.

Holiday was amused by all this. He knew these grunts were sending a message to the "in the rear with the gear" gang, announcing through their actions how good they had it, and they were not perturbed by melting ice cream and that they had not had a hot meal other than c-rations cooked over a heat tab for quite a long time. It was a deliberate gross out, a slap at the whiners and complainers who did not appreciate what they DID have.

Towards the end of their meal, as they all started to burp loudly, Holiday got up and handing a napkin to the one grunt, said, " Uh, you have a little bit of mashed potatoes in your moustache there , marine." Without looking up, the grunt took the napkin, daintily tapped at the corners of his mouth, then proceeded to insert the napkin into his mouth.

"Dessert?" Holiday inquired. A loud burp answered him with a "yup" "Glad you enjoyed our dining facilities, please feel free to return at any time and treat yourself to our cuisine. Lima Co 3/7, you?" The grunt looking at him in the eyes for the first time, recognizing the "look" that all combat veterans had looking back at him, a slight smile creeping onto his lips, replied "Foxtrot, 2/4". Standing up, grabbing his helmet and m-16, grunted "move out" to his buddies and off they went.

Roberts, watching this interchange, began to grumble, "There was no need to act like that, like pigs, like animals..........." "Yes, there was," Holiday interjected. He and Roberts spent the next hour in the PX, where Holiday spent some military script on toilet articles and a couple of cartons of cigarettes, before saying his good-byes.

He began trying to hitch rides to battalion HQ. 1500 that afternoon found him waiting in a village off of route 4. While waiting, Holiday noticed a bunch of PF soldiers acting as sentries for this vil. There were a few other marines trying to hitch back to their units as well. Tired of standing, Holiday sat down next to a PF who had his weapon on his lap, leaning against a stone hutch, just 20 feet from the road. Holiday tried to strike up a conversation with this soldier, but the PF never would look at him. He seemed intent on watching a group of kids playing about 30 feet away from where they both were sitting.

Suddenly the PF raised his weapon and shouldering it, aimed at and shot a young boy who had a basket of cokes draped on his arm. The boy crumpled, dead, before he hit the ground. Shocked, Holiday turned to the soldier, but before he could say anything, the PF had jumped to his feet and in broken English, was saying "No here, no here" (not from here) "Look" and crouching down, turned the basket towards Holiday, gingerly removed a couple of cokes from the basket to reveal grenades, American grenades, pins almost entirely pulled out. The boy had been approaching the marines waiting for rides as if to sell them the 8 oz. bottled cokes, with the intent, not apparent, of fragging the marines as they gathered around to buy the cokes.

"How did you know? Holiday inquired. A boy of about 13 or 14 said in better English than the PF was capable of, that this boy was not from this village, that the PF knew this and had been watching him and knew as he approached the marines what his intent had been. "But why kill him?" The boy, translating, asked Holiday, how else was he to be stopped? How else indeed!

This is a nasty war, where kids are sent to kill Americans through deceit, not in combat, but in situations that would be

considered safe or normal in appearance. Kids! Women too!
These people are animals, sending their kids to die.

Holiday's heart hardened just that much more after this incident. People back home will never understand. He wondered, if he ever made it back alive, what would he be able to tell people about this place

11 Nov :67 . Veterans day today. Back on hill 37 Battalion HQ. Saw the battalion CO dress down India Company for looking raggedy. I guess the CO thinks Mickey Mouse needs to be alive and well even over here. Saw a stateside cpl get laughed at for trying to push Mickey Mouse on a marine today, too. I just don't get it. They are more concerned with appearance than in getting the job done? They want to assert their authority? They think military decorum keeps us military? Don't THEY get it? I obey orders because I respect the man, not his rank. And most marines are the same way. The other day a 90 day wonder funewgy lieutenant told us to charge a vil. We just snickered at him and strolled in. The LT didn't know to shit or go blind. Military decorum is a joke in a combat zone. These Remington Raiders need to spend some time in the bush, get attacked by an army of red ants, have leeches covering them, scorpions crawl over them, lie in water for hours under fire, see their buddies get blown away, carry a dead marine to a chopper under fire, be so scared you shit in your pants. But to them, having a button unbuttoned is a big deal. I understand why those gyrenes got gross while eating in the mess hall when I was in Danang. You pull a wounded marine out of the line of fire not because you are ordered to, but because you want him to do the same for you and you want him to live.

You obey orders not because you fear negative consequences but because you trust the man giving the order. You take chances because you are proud of your unit, your buddies, not because some second lewy says to. Gunny Marshall is lucky to be alive, that bastard. He has been in combat and he still doesn't get it.

Holiday had time to relax while waiting for a chopper flight back to his hill. He had made it back from Da Nang via convoy and had heard that a chopper was scheduled to fly from HQ to Hill 52 later on that day. He appreciated Sgt Mueller letting him take a few days off and getting away for a few days. Holiday was feeling very tired. He had seen too much, been through too much. At 19, he was feeling like an old man

Battalion HQ was situated on a hill that had a stone fort built there by the French many years ago. Holiday had chosen a place on the wall that overlooked the lowlands for miles, to sit and write in his journal. One could almost see the coast from where he was perched. The world, his world, was peaceful for the moment. There were no clouds of dust from explosions anywhere on the horizon. No noise of combat, not even the sounds of choppers flying about. There was a slight breeze pushing puffy white clouds lazily through the sky.

His heart was heavy in his chest from memories of the day Charlie died. This was pushed away by the anger he felt for those men who seem to value decorum and protocol over the lives of the men. He had left H&S CO office and saw India Company in formation on the so-called parade ground. He knew they had just come back from a nasty operation that had left many dead and more wounded. He overheard the Colonel berating them for needing haircuts, for having muddy boots and torn uniforms, needing shaves. He heard him explain that they must look like marines and not a bunch of animals. Holiday noticed the empty look in the eyes of these men, most not over the age of 21. He knew that look; the look of seeing death, causing death, watching buddies die, the look of weariness, of hiding fear and pain; and this bird colonel was lecturing them on their appearance. My god!

There was a private standing next to him, an acquaintance Holiday knew from one of the platoons in Lima Company. A grunt who had seen too much. As was the custom of marines in the bush, his utility shirt was unbuttoned, to allow the breeze to help cool off the body. Standard uniform was a green T shirt under a buttoned jungle utility shirt, with sleeves rolled up 4 times to above the elbow. This marine had his hands in his pockets (a no no) and his trousers were unbloused (no ankle band to tuck in the ends just above the boots) He was wearing well-worn jungle boots, that were caked in dry mud, his hair was unkempt and he needed a shave. Holiday learned later that he had just come out of office hours, and been busted to private for drinking a beer while on watch.. He could have gotten brig time for that offense, but good, experienced combat marines were hard to replace.

Out of the corner of his eye, Holiday noticed a stateside marine approaching the private. Apparently, inspired by the colonels speech, decided he was going to dress down the private on his appearance. This corporal was dressed in stateside utilities, still wearing the black leather boots instead of jungle boots, and wearing a white T shirt with his cover (hat) starched, as was typical for marines in the states.

"You are out of uniform, where are your chevrons?" he spoke to the private. "I'm wearing them," was the retort. (Privates do not have chevrons, private first class have one stripe)

"You need to button your shirt and blouse your boots…."

"You need to back off, corporal" Holiday interjected. Holiday had his lance corporal chevrons on his collar, out ranked by the funewgy. "You are talking to a marine who outranks you….." Holiday bust out laughing. "What are you going to do, Cpl, send me to Nam?" It was the private's turn to bust out laughing.

"Stow your chickenshit attitude, Cpl," Holiday continued. "Over here we don't even salute officers once you are off this hill. C'mon private, I'll buy you a beer" Holiday said as he started to walk away from the funewgy. "Oh, and Cpl?….Everyone here carries a weapon. I'd keep that in mind the next time you feel froggy and want to jump a grunt's ass" The private snickered as they both sauntered off in the general direction of the mess hall.

> 12 Nov: 67 Four marines got blown away last night. I am still at Battalion. I missed the flight back to my hill when I went to the messhall. Seems the bridge security on the north side of the hill, were all smoking pot and the gooks just walked up to them around dusk last evening and blew them away. The guys were so stoned that they didn't bother to think these men might be armed. The marines on the south side of the bridge saw everything, but the weapons had been hid until just as they pulled them out and wasted all 4 marines on the far side of the bridge. The other guys could not react quick enough before the gooks ran off into the paddies . I have been ordered to go out on a sparrow hawk tonight to patrol close to some of our CAP units. Seems the skipper thinks the gooks might try something with them since they had the balls to surprise the bridge security. But why me? I am with Lima CO. Why can't they use their own FO and radioman?

"Holiday, you're with me tonight" spoke a young tall Cpl to Holiday as he sat on a bunk cleaning his .45. "Who the hell are you and where are we going? Holiday enquired. "My name's Johnson and I am Mike CO's FO." "Where is your radioman…" "Dead" came the quick and matter of fact reply.

Holiday said no more. He knew this man must be hurting, losing his radioman, like he had lost Charlie. There was an unwritten rule among the grunts.

Whenever a comrade got killed, that night, if there was an opportunity, all the men would talk about the dead man, like an informal eulogy. Once they were talked out, it seemed that the dead man's name was never mentioned again. No one could afford to harbor pain for the dead. It was enough to try and stay alive yourself. However, for the one closest to the fallen buddy, he learned to carry his pain silently. Holiday could see Johnson was carrying his pain for his dead radioman. Holiday respected that and knew enough to not ask how he died or say something stupid, like, was he your friend? If Johnson wanted to talk about it he would, but Holiday knew from his own experience, one does not share that pain with a comrade. One keeps it to himself. For tomorrow it may be your turn to die.

The patrol that night was 2nd platoon, Mike Company, headed up by a lifer named Marshall. The platoon knew Holiday was FO and radioman for Lima Company. They had heard about him refusing to go out in the bush with a new FO, having lost Charlie and then Goodwin (wounded) and liked the idea that this patrol would have 2 qualified FO's, Johnson and Holiday. Several grunts had approached Holiday to grumble and complain about Marshall, how he cared little for his troops, made stupid decisions in the bush that had on occasion jeopardized lives unnecessarily, and was, in their words, an asshole.

"Alright you morons, saddle up" Marshall spit out. "See what I mean," whispered a grunt in Holiday's ear.

The sun was starting to set as they traveled along a river bank, headed towards a CAP unit a few vils to the east. The bank had been cut into by the river so that the river itself was about 4 feet straight down from the bank. Following it was an easy jaunt, until it got dark. It got SO dark, as it does in Nam, that one could not see one's own hand 5 inches in front of one's face, yet the sarge, kept following the river. It came as no surprise that 2 grunts slipped and fell the four feet into the river. Marshall's response was to call the two men morons, which seemed to be the only 2 syllable word the Sarge knew.

After what seemed an eternity, the gunny called a halt. They had been walking for hours. Holiday suspected the gunny had over shot his goal and had decided to bivouac for the night. It beat stumbling around lost at night in enemy territory, but it seemed the gunny was either too proud or too scared to radio back to HQ and ask for directions.

The place Marshall had chosen was not good. The river had cut into the bank, receded and left a sandy area. To the north was the new bank, still about 4 feet above the level of the river, and to the south was the river itself. Holiday, who was used to trying to set up night defensive fires in case of ambush, had not had the opportunity to do so, not having enough light to view his map. Marshall had marched them half the night and even he did not know where they were. If the gooks attacked from the dry ground, they had their backs to the river and would be massacred like animals brought to a slaughterhouse. With their backs to the river, a rather fast moving river, there was no cover and no where to go. If the gooks attacked from across the river, the marines had their backs literally against a wall of dirt and had no place to go. Apparently Marshall had chosen this site because the sand was soft to sleep on compared to the hard ground everywhere else.

Holiday was nervous, more nervous than usual. This lifer had gotten a platoon lost and had set up bivouac in a dangerous place and Holiday, not knowing where they were could not set up defensive fire zones and would not be able to call in 81 support at all, were they to get hit. Marshall had TWO experienced FO's in his patrol and had rendered them useless. "What the fuck is this? Holiday whispered to Johnson, referring to the gunny's decision to bivouac here. "Typical", whispered back Johnson, the disgust in his voice not easily hidden.

Holiday hunkered down for the night, finding it difficult to get any sleep. Every noise woke him up. A grunt on watch had crawled up to Holiday. "Relax" he whispered. "We go through this stupid shit with him every time we pull night patrols." Holiday appreciated the assurance from a grunt his own age and not corrupted by the power that comes with rank, like the gunny. Holiday finally drifted off into a restless sleep.

> 13 Nov:67 Gunny Marshall got "accidentally shot in the ass, that puke. About 2 weeks before that he almost got shot dead by his own men.

Holiday woke up with a start. He was completely awake and alert. He heard noises coming from about 4 feet away. Another marine was awake, probably as scared as he was, thought Holiday. Holiday fumbled for his red lensed flashlight to catch a glimpse of the time on his watch. Nearly 0400 and still pitch black. Suddenly Holiday saw a blue glow from the marine he had heard fumbling around. That bastard had lit a heat tab to make coffee. Jesus Christ! Any gook within a mile would see that glow. Holiday scrambled over to the heat tab and kicked it into the sand stomping on it with his boot, trying to bury it in the ground.

"And what the fuck do you think you are doing?" Holiday heard the twang from Marshall.

"Putting out the sniper light, you moron." Holiday had used that term deliberately. "That is MY, Gunny Marshall's coffee you just kicked over, MORON. I'll bust your ass for this."

In the dark both Marshall and Holiday heard the sound of a round being chambered in an M-16. Then a loud whisper of a grunt, "No you won't Sarge". The implication was obvious. "Who is that?" Marshall asked. Immediately 2 more rifles were heard to chamber rounds. "No one Sarge", another voice was heard, "just your imagination." Gunny became very quiet and motionless.

"I can see why the guys hate your guts, Gunny," Holiday whispered to Marshall. "I suggest you have your lifer juice later one when the sun is up." Marshall said nothing, but Holiday was sure Marshall would try to get him back at some point. Holiday figured he was too dumb to catch the hint his troops were giving him by chambering their rounds, and would plot his revenge.

Holiday needn't have worried. Later on that day an event happened that took Marshall out of the bush, for about 2 months.

Being TAD (temporary assigned duty) to Mike company for this patrol, Holiday had managed to "borrow" an M-14. He had always felt that a .45 was not enough firepower, even though his .45 had saved his life on several occasions.

Marshall had them wandering around the countryside for half of the morning, still not having found a CAP (Combined Action Platoon) unit. But Holiday had managed to see his map once daylight had come and had had a grunt show him where he thought the CAP unit was. Holiday kept this information to himself. He, as well as the rest of the patrol were enjoying watching Marshall, obviously lost, trying to act like he knew what he was doing. It was a running joke for the day, getting Marshall more lost. "Why don't we try that area, Gunny, Holiday heard a Cpl tell Marshall with a straight face. "We haven't been there yet."

Holiday agreed with the other grunts to see if they could get Marshall to take the patrol in a huge circle all around the CAP unit, to see if he would ever catch on what they were doing. It kept the grunts in high spirits all morning, watching Marshall make a fool of himself, trying to find the CAP unit while everyone else knew they had been patrolling all around it.

They were approaching a vil. As usual the platoon was walking single file, as they wound their way through the vil. Holiday noticed that many of the villagers were in the rice patties plowing, using their water buffaloes. As Holiday's section of the column was about to make it out of the village, he heard Marshall say,"Ah recognize this here area," . "If'n we cut across this paddy we will be right close to the CAP." And off he went, yelling at the patrol to follow him. The grunts fell into single file behind him, following him across the paddy. Holiday kept back, not wanting to be anywhere near this lifer, content to hang with some of the grunts in the middle of the file.

BLAM BLAM! Holiday's heart jumped in his chest. *"That sounded like an M-16"*....It was! Holiday could see Marshall sprinting across the rice paddy with a water Bo close behind him. Apparently the water buffalo had broken from its yoke and was chasing him. Water buffalos were notorious for hating the smell of American meat eaters. Holiday swung his M–14 up to his shoulder, taking a bead on the waterbo, he then changed his site to follow Marshall running from right to left about 50 yards front of him. While one or two marines shot at the water Bo to stop him, Holiday pulled the trigger aiming at Marshall's ass. A cheer from the marines told him his shot was true to the mark.

Racing up to see his handiwork, Holiday saw Marshall writhing in agony cursing out whoever that dumbass marine was who shot him instead of the water bo. Holiday leaned over Marshall, who was on the ground holding his hand over a hole in his ass. "Gee, Gunny, I must be a bad shot" Several marines snickered. Holiday could see Marshall's mind working. Was he a bad shot that he got him instead of the water bo or a bad shot that he didn't kill him but only wounded him in the buttocks. Holiday smiled a sweet smile, put the barrel of the rifle to his lips and blew the smoke away like a cowboy would do with his pistol after a gunfight. The marines snickered again. "Someone call in a medevac," one grunt said. "Oh, and Gunny, I wouldn't put anything in your report except to say, Holiday here was

trying to shoot the water bo to save your ass...........
because that is what we will all swear to." Marshall saw
every marine nod his head in agreement.

Holiday knew he would be safe from Marshall now. He
would not be around to use the rules to set him up and,
Holiday thought, he had just made friends with every
man in 2nd platoon Mike Company.

As Holiday's time in country lengthened, he was
unaware of the change in his attitude and demeanor.
He could not see that his outlook on life had hardened,
or that his distrust for those in authority had grown
cynical. He could see the need for rules and regulations,
for without them there would be chaos and with
them, goals would be accomplished, order would be
maintained, but when rules were rigid, it seemed the
rules became more important than the purpose for the
rules. Rules are created to try and govern behavior and
to try and ensure fairness for all. Add in the factor that
the enforcers of rules are human and as such the power
of enforcing the rules can and does go to their heads.
When this happens, people get hurt or killed.

> 14 Nov:67 Back on Hill 52. The guys were having rat
> shooting contests. Prescott was the best gunner we have
> on 81's and he proved it with his distance and accuracy
> shooting those rats out of the tubes. The centipedes are
> worse than the rats and the snakes are worse than the
> centipedes.. The red ants hurt like hell, but those snakes
> can kill you in seconds. I don't like the scorpions too
> much either. Had one run across my body a couple of

times one night Almost drank one once. I don't know which is deadlier, the red or the black ones. The leaches are a pain too. Once while crossing a river, I came out on the other side covered in leeches. It took forever to burn them off my body. I hate those snakes the most. Especially the human kind. I remember that one time that young chick set me up. Hell, she would have been happy had anyone of us gotten blown away by that booby trap. I do not like Sgt Flowers any more.

"Saddle up" Holiday was getting tired of hearing that phrase. It meant he was going on patrol yet again. It seemed every squad, platoon and fire team wanted him on their patrols.

At least the day was cool, relatively speaking, the skies were partly cloudy and the breeze was enough to keep the marines from being instantly saturated with sweat.

This patrol was platoon size, Lt Forester headed up the second platoon. He was a quiet man but was well respected by his men. He seemed to have a handle on guerilla tactics and was very good at setting up ambushes and avoiding ambushes sprung on the marines by the enemy.

They were approaching a vil. The patrol was snaking through the trees, He could see the snake weaving in and out of the trees when he noticed the pattern had changed; from skirting to the right side of a huge tree to now taking a path to the left….why? Scanning to the left of the tree he saw the most beautiful young woman he had ever seen since coming to Nam. Holiday found Vietnamese women to be sexy anyway, with their long shiny black hair, olive colored smooth skin, almond shaped eyes and perfectly proportioned bodies, but this girl was absolutely gorgeous. So…like every other red blooded American horny 19 year old stud, he skirted to the left of that huge tree, to get a closer look.

Holiday was so enamored with her beauty; he did not notice the coldness in her eyes until he heard the click above his head. Quickly looking up, he saw the blue wisp of smoke coming out of a grenade that his antenna had tripped just above his head. Ducking his head, and hoping his radio would protect him he sprinted as fast as he could trying to put distance between himself and that booby trap. No explosion! A dud.

"Where the hell are you going Marine? Do you think someone called you for chow?" the LT inquired. The young beauty was nowhere to be seen. Holiday told the LT about the booby trap. Instantly the LT knew this was not a friendly vil and that we may expect an ambush once we cleared the vil. It was then that Holiday realized he had seen only women, children and old men in this vil. Damn! An ambush was almost a certainty.

It was getting dark; LT would have to pick a bivouac soon. This was a platoon sized patrol. Holiday always felt "safer" with a platoon. Usually they would be sniped at, but hardly ever ambushed. It was those squad or fire team sized patrols that scared the shit out of him.

The lieutenant had found the stand of trees, mostly bamboo, to bivouac his platoon in. The night passed without incident. Holiday had felt certain there would've been an ambush that night. The platoon began to stagger out of the stand of trees in single file. What was ahead of them were acres of rice patties. Holiday could see in the distance a few hooches on elevated ground about 120 yards ahead of them. The point man gave the signal to halt and jogged back to talk the lieutenant. The lieutenant called for an online sweep. This is essentially a column turned 90°.

Apparently, the point man had told the lieutenant something that prompted the lieutenant to call for the sweep. Sure enough, after about 40 yards of sweeping, a machine gun opened up on them. Everybody hit the deck. As the Marines returned fire, Holiday noticed Cpl. Perkins from North Carolina headed towards the enemy fire, he had been the furthest Marine to the left of the line. The enemy did not notice him running towards the elevated ground. As the Marines continued the firefight, Holiday saw Perkins crawl on his hands and knees using the wall of the elevated ground as cover.

Holiday had always thought Perkins was a bit crazy. What he saw next confirmed this. Perkins had made it to the machine gun and sitting directly beneath it, he waved at the Marines smiling the whole time. Perkins was giving hand signals indicating that he was going to pull the barrel of the machine gun down, there-by halting the barrage of bullets. We knew if he succeeded, we would rush the position.

One of the scariest aspects of a firefight is to be pinned down with no cover. Still smiling, Perkins signaled that on the count of three, he would yank the barrel of the machine gun. One... two... three! From a sitting position, Perkins extended his hands grabbed the barrel and yanked down hard. This motion knocked both the gunner and "A" gunner away from the machine gun. The "A" gunner stood up to shoot him and was immediately cut down by a Marine's bullet. Meanwhile, Perkins had scrambled to his feet and ran a short distance after the gunner and tackled the VC.

By this time the Marines had rushed the position. There had been only three VC and two of them were dead. It seems the VC had depended on the stolen M-60 machine gun to do the work of a larger VC force. The M-60 had probably come off of a downed chopper.

"Well looky here, ol' Perkins captured himself a woman" snorted one of the grunts. "No woman" Sgt Flowers retorted, "her VC". The lieutenant had brought along Flowers on this patrol because they had gone into a new area and none of the grunts knew if any of the locals could speak American.

Flowers approached the woman, who was still being bear hugged by Perkins. Another grunt had "volunteered" to hold her on one side while Perkins held her on the other.

Flowers squatted down and began interrogating the prisoner in his harsh manner. The woman, no older than 25 spit in his face. Flowers stood up and without a word, went over to a stand of bamboo and cut himself an 8 foot length of a 2 inch diameter stalk and with his K bar, cut a point at the tip. Walking casually back to the woman he placed the bamboo pole between her legs and in English, shouted "You talk". The woman spit in his face again. Immediately Flowers punched her in the mouth and shouted, "Talk" She spit blood in his face. Flowers jammed that pole up between her legs as the Marines watched in horror. "Lieutenant?" a Marine had pleaded. "He is not a Marine. I cannot do anything. In fact, we are under strict orders not to interfere when a Vietnamese national is interrogating a POW". "This isn't an interrogation, this is torture and murder"..."As you were Marine", LT shouted. Flowers stood up, faced the Lieutenant and said, "She die now".

Flowers dragged the screaming woman to the edge of the dry land where it dropped off into the rice paddy, with the bamboo pole still lodged up her vagina. Grabbing her shirt he wretched her in an upright position and helped the pole set itself in the paddy mud. The marines watched in horror as her body slowly sank deeper on the pole. Soon, but not soon enough, her screams stopped and her body went limp.

The ensuing silence was deafening. All those battle hardened marines were in a state of shock. They could not believe what they had just seen. Most knew Flowers had had his father murdered by the VC in front of his eyes and they knew the hate he had for them. But no one had ever imagined that this "ally" would be as cruel and callous as they had just witnessed. What made it even more eerie was the fact that Sgt Flowers was a well-mannered, soft spoken, educated young man.

Holiday was caught in a moral dilemma. He had viewed this war as a conflict between good and evil, with himself as one of the good guys. This incident had rattled him to his very core. But he could not afford to analyze this and question right or wrong. He, like every other marine, was focused on surviving and helping his buddies survive. Perhaps at a later date, far from this hell hole; but not now. He could not.

> 6 Dec: 67 We flew out to Elephant Valley today. Chased those gooks all day. The only thing we killed was a water buffalo. He must have been VC. He attacked me.

Holiday heard choppers. Looking up he saw 2 CH-46 helicopters heading towards the hill. These choppers were used as troop transports and supply vehicles. Two squads from first platoon were forming up at the LZ. "Grab your gear, Holiday, you are coming with us" Without hesitation, Holiday jogged back to his hooch, grabbed his radio, strapped on his .45 and a sock and a pack of C rations. His pistol belt always had a canteen and small first aid kit attached. He shook his canteen... yep, full.

His new FO, a marine named Plum was already at the LZ waiting for him. S/Sgt Mattie was pointing at Plum to get into the first chopper. A CH 46 had a rear hatch that drops down like a ramp. Holiday ran up the ramp and grabbed the first empty canvas seat he could. As Plum sat next to him, Holiday yelled in his ear, "Where we going?" Plum shrugged and shouted back, over the din of the engines and chopper blades, "Fuck if I know" Holiday opened up his C rations and began stuffing cans of food into his sock. Motioning to Plum, he had Plum tie the sock to his radio. "You bring any chow?" ask Holiday. With another shrug and a sheepish grin, Plum yells, "No"

The chopper lifted off from the LZ and began circling the hill waiting for the other chopper to load up. Holiday had mixed emotions about flying in choppers. He enjoyed the view and it sure beat walking for miles in 110 degree weather, but usually a flight meant going into imminent combat. Holiday spent the next few minutes gearing his mind for a firefight.

When one knows he is about to see or cause death, the first thing one does is convince himself it won't be him. Were he not to do this, panic would ensue and panic can kill. Panic grips the mind; all the training, all the experience of previous battles gets lost. Fear then becomes the controller. Panic IS uncontrolled fear. So, Holiday, like most combat Marines, tells himself, it will not be him who dies. Even so, he tries to prepare himself for death, were it to come.

Over the din of the engines, Holiday could hear pings. Looking around he saw holes in the deck that were not there an instant before. The first instinct when being fired at is to "hit the deck", but in this case "hitting the deck" would expose ones entire body to bullets coming UP instead of AT one. Holiday yelled as loud as he could to get the other marine's attention, pointing at the new holes being made in the deck of the CH-46. Every grunt pushed his body as far back in his seat as he could hoping none of the bullets would enter the chopper from the side. It is most terrifying when one feels so helpless and at the mercy of fate or God.

Holiday could feel the chopper bank hard to the left and lose altitude. They were going in. Elephant Valley got its name from the elephant grass that nearly covered the entire valley; grass that grew upwards of 10 feet, very thick and tough grass that cut like razors.

The chopper leveled off at about 10-12 feet and the rear

ramp came down. No way could the bird land with this type of vegetation. Marines started towards the rear hatch, the door gunner began kicking the grunts in the ass to force them to jump....into the unknown. Holiday pulled out his .45. When it became his turn to stand at the end of the ramp, he quickly spun and pointing his pistol into the face of the door gunner, yelled, "Don't kick me, asshole". Looking down, he made sure it was clear to jump, not wanting to land on the previous man who had jumped just before him, he turned to the door gunner, smiled and yelled, "Have a nice day" and leaped off backwards. It was a hard landing, especially since he was wearing that damn 30 pound radio.

S/Sgt Mattie motioned for Holiday to come up to him. "You stick with me, Holiday." Holiday realized, with the elephant grass so high and thick, were there to be a firefight, it would be like shooting blind and mortars were an effective weapon in such terrain. "Uh, Sarge.... we have a problem. We are out of range for mortars off of hill 52."

"Well, shit, contact a closer hill," was the retort. "Uh... Sarge, I do not know what outfit is close nor do I know their frequencies and Battalion will not give out a frequency, even though the gooks are probably monitoring all of our frequencies". With a look of disgust, Mattie muttered, "You are about as useful as a handle on a pisspot" then calling for another Marine, ordered him to take point and head us down to the nearest vil, assuming that whoever shot at us had either headed for the higher elevations or the villages. The safe bet was to head for the vils, hoping to get closer to any kind of artillery support should the need arise.

Within a hour the patrol had made it out of the hills and was passing through the first vil, in single file as was the custom. Holiday, as usual, linked up with a fire team close to the middle of the column. He could see the front of the column had already made it out of the vil and was heading towards the next, when from a paddy, came a water buffalo charging at every Marine he could see. As the Marines scattered, the "bo" charged straight on and was headed right towards Holiday. Holiday quickly pulled out his .45 and attempted to chamber a round when the slide jammed. Backing up and in a near panic, he kept slamming the slide with the heel of his hand, hoping to unjam it before the water buffalo caught up to him.

From behind, he heard the LAW (Light Anti-Tank) man yell, "HIT THE DECK" Immediately crouching down, Holiday heard a click then whoosh as the round from the LAW passed right over his head, striking the waterbo head on. Pieces of that buffalo went flying everywhere. Turning on his heels to look at the LAW man, he saw a big grin and wink. "Jesus H Christ! That LAW could have torn me a new asshole, it was so close" "Nah" came the reply. "He was far enough away where the shrapnel wouldn't have gotcha" "And anyway, it got the job done". Still grinning, he motioned to Holiday to move out.

Each vil the Marines moved through was searched for weapons and IDs were checked. By the time it started to get dark, the patrol had made it to a Marine Unit just off of Rte. 4. A convoy of 5x5 trucks awaited them to drive them back to their own hill.

> 14 Dec: 67 We captured the local VC tax collector. Bun, a 14 yr old boy, who liked everything American, was the boy who turned him in. Everyone had been afraid of this tax collector because he was also acting as a spy for the VC and would intimidate local villagers to extract information. From what I could gather from Bun, the taxman had had one of Bun's relatives executed for refusing to cooperate and Bun wanted revenge.

Holiday had gone to the bottom of the hill where the bamboo constructed "store and barbershop" was. His unit was so far out from other units, that this store was a welcome addition to the village, since they sold 8 oz. cokes, bags of chips and non-chocolate candy. Capitalism in action, right here in Vietnam. The barber was not so bad either. For a few extra piasters (money) one could get a back massage as well as a haircut.

After shaking his coke and holding it up to the sun to see if any glass was floating around inside the bottle, Holiday popped the top and took a swig. Holiday saw Bun approaching but without his entourage of other boys accompanying him. Holiday bought another coke and handed it to Bun. With a swig of the coke, Bun motioned Holiday to sit down. Whispering in his ear, Bun told him about the tax collector and why he wanted to turn him in and offered to show him where the VC lived.

Holiday grabbed another marine and started down the path towards the West side of the vil. Hearing footsteps running behind him, Holiday turned to see Sgt. Flowers. *Shit!* "*I am not going to stand by and watch this animal torture anyone*" thought Holiday. "We don't want you to come along" Holiday stated matter of factually. "You speak Vietnamese?" inquired Flowers. "*Well, hell, he had me there,*" thought Holiday. Turning back towards the interior of the vil, Holiday motioned Bun to lead the way.

About 200 yards down the path, Bun turned north. About 30 yards up, Bun pointed to bamboo hooch to the right front and quickly disappeared. Scoping out the hooch, the two marines and Flowers found no one. Probably still out in the paddies, thought Holiday. "You stay here with Flowers" Holiday said to the other grunt. I'll go back and get a snoopy team. If he comes back, arrest him and don't let Flowers interrogate him" "It will be dark soon. Keep a candle lit. If the candle is still on when we get back, we will know you are OK." Holiday explained to the other marine that if the taxman came back with VC friends they would be outnumbered and out gunned. The real reason was

Holiday did not want to have to shoot Flowers if he refused to stop torturing a captured VC.

Holiday immediately reported to the Captain when he got back to the hill. The Captain assembled a snoopy team and gave orders to capture and return and leave interrogation to an American Interpreter. The Captain was aware of the incident with Flowers with the female machine gunner, but for as much as he loathed Flowers he had been ordered to use Flowers.

A Snoopy team is usually a fire team used to reconnoiter and capture suspected VC. They did not wear helmets or flak jackets, and usually did not bring a radio with them. The key to their success was stealth, thus no radio and nothing that may make noise or slow them down. They would sneak off the hill at night, go to a vil and either kidnap a suspected VC or watch and monitor any unusual activities going on in a vil that should be asleep. Many of these patrols would come back with information that determined future search and destroy missions. Rumor was that operation Arizona was initiated due to several snoopy team reports.

Holiday and the 4 snoopy team members hurried off the hill and back towards where Holiday had left the grunt and Sgt Flowers. By now it was dark, so Holiday expected to see the candle lit. It was not.

In fact there were no candles lit in any of the hooches and it had just gotten dark. This was unusual. Standing about 40 feet from the hooch entrance, Cpl Diaz, the team leader motioned Holiday to sweep around the hooch, gather any pertinent info and report back to him. Holiday started moving to the right, going as silently as he could, when he heard a grunt. Immediately dropping to his knees and with his heart in his throat, aimed his .45 at the sound, pressure on the trigger. Peering through the darkness, he could barely make out the outline of a very large sow, suckling about a dozen piglets about 6 feet to his left. Relieved that he had not shot the pig and given away his position were there any VC in the area, Holiday got back to his feet and continued to circle around to the backside of the hooch.

Holiday found himself hugging the outside wall of the hutch when he heard and felt heavy breathing on his neck. He realized he had crept between the hooch and the stall where a water Bo was housed. That breathing was from an angry buffalo. Backing away from the Bo, Holiday continued down the wall when his foot pushed against a body.

Quickly kneeling down and with pistol pointed at the body, (just in case) Holiday nudged it. Holiday was hoping he had not stumbled onto a dead marine's body. Holiday's mind was racing; were it a dead marine it meant the VC were here, had killed him and either were waiting in ambush, or had killed and/or captured Flowers and had left the area.

Groping with his left hand, Holiday felt the face, warm...
and stirring. "Wha?" muttered the half-awake grunt.
Holiday cupped his hand over his mouth and whispered
"Shut up" "Why isn't the candle lit, where is Flowers
and what the hell are you doing out here sleeping?"

"You took too long, so I came out here to wait. I must
have dozed off. And I don't know where Flowers is."
Holiday stood up, yanked the grunt to his feet and
completed circling the hooch. When he got to the
doorway, he saw the candle was lit and 4 marines were
standing there. Diaz said, "No Flowers, no VC taxman
and what the fuck took you so long?" "I had to wake
up sleeping beauty here," was the retort.

Diaz ordered the team to roust the inhabitants. Most
of these hooches had built a bunker underground in
the middle of the main room, for protection against
bombs. In a village this size all floors were dirt. Most
had straw mats or actual throw carpets laid down in
heavy traffic areas. During the monsoon season that
mud got cold and these peasants either wore nothing
on their feet or sandals. A warm dry carpet on cold wet
mud was a luxury.

After rousting all the people Diaz, who for this mission
had brought a radio, called back in saying they could
find no taxman and Flowers was missing. They were
ordered to stay where they were at, that a platoon was
coming down to get them. The hill had gotten a report

176

from the Green Beret post 6 miles to the West that their snoopy team had seen hundreds of VC approaching their vil from the West. Minimum number was 200.

Shit! Six Marines to ward off 200 gooks! Yeah, send that platoon. The immediate problem is the army had lost track of the VC and had no idea how close they were to the vil.

Just then, a baby started to cry. "Shut that kid up, Diaz ordered. The mother was trying rock her baby, as mothers do, but to no avail. One of the marines interpreted her bouncing the baby up and down as trying to agitate the baby to get it to cry more and give away their position. With a balled fist, he punched the baby, then grabbed the woman and clamping his hand over her mouth to stifle her scream, whispered harshly. "You bitch, you are making that baby cry more" Another marine clamped his hand over the other's bayonet scabbard to stop him from pulling it to cut the woman's throat. "Jesus Christ" snarled Diaz. That baby is quiet now. Knock it off" He took a quick look at the baby to see if it was still alive, when a third marine whispered loudly, "Diaz, come here"

There was a straw mat placed UNDER a dresser. Were it a chest it would make sense to protect the bottom of the chest from mud, but this dresser had 4 skinny legs, so why was the mat under the dresser and not in front of it? "Pull that dresser away". As the dresser was removed,

Diaz stood to the side, his rifle pointed at the mat. The mat was ripped away and lo and behold, there crouched the tax man. One marine pulled him out by his hair. Diaz whispers "Call this in and ask for orders"

Holiday had watched all this unfold. In 10 minutes, Holiday had almost shot a pig, a water buffalo and a sleeping Marine. Within the last 10 minutes, Holiday had watched a baby get punched, a VC get captured and heard a radio report that said at least 200 VC were coming through the vil.

Then Holiday heard it. It sounded like crackling thunder. It was an empty illumination canister falling from the sky and landing not more than 50 feet away. Nothing like announcing to the VC we are here, thought Holiday. The last message from the hill was to stay put, they were sending a platoon to come and get them. Once one illumination was burned out, another was fired. Each round lit up the sky as each canister crashed very close to them. The guns were firing their maximum distance to try and light up the vil, more to see if they could catch the VC and also to slow down their advance. As each minute passed, Holiday became more anxious. *"We are 6 marines, one prisoner and no Sgt Flowers",* thought Holiday.

After a few more anxious minutes, they were radioed the order to move back towards the hill. As each illumination round exploded overhead, the grunts would hit the deck and wait until night came back; then they would hurriedly travel down the path, hoping to get to the main trail before the oncoming VC. Finally they reached the main trail. Holiday radioed the platoon and told them with the next illumination round he would stand up and holler for them and to PLEASE not shoot him. His gamble was the marines were closer to him than the VC. Diaz told him it was an excellent idea, and that he, Holiday was crazy to do it. Semper Fi.

As the next round burst overhead, Holiday jumped into the main path and yelled "DON"T SHOOT"! He saw the entire platoon raise their rifles to their shoulders about 40 yards up the path. For an instant, Holiday pictured a dozen bullet holes piercing his body from the front. In the next instant he pictured a dozen bullets piercing his back from the VC. After letting go of his breath, he turned to the other marines and said "Let's go".

As he got closer to the other grunts, he noticed Sgt Flowers standing to the side. Anger welled up in his chest. That pussy bastard had run and hid instead of waiting. If that damn sleeping beauty had stayed awake, both he and Flowers could have captured the tax man by themselves and all of this could have been avoided.

Holiday sneered at Flowers. "Where the hell did you go?" Flowers, sheepishly muttered. "I think you leave me so I come back." "We are United States Marines, we do not run and we do not abandon our allies." Holiday saw the Lieutenant smile, even in the darkness. "Holiday, escort our prisoner to the hill." "Sgt Flowers," he continued, "You have had a rough day, so our man will interrogate" pointing to Sgt Jacobson, who knew Vietnamese. "You are relieved". The lieutenant had heard what Flowers had done to that female machine gunner and did not want Flowers on his hill nor wanted him to do any more interrogations. It was shortly afterwards that Flowers asked for a transfer. No one was sorry to see him go.

Holiday did as he was ordered and escorted the prisoner to hooch. Sgt. Jacobson started asking him questions, but the tax man stayed silent. Rather than use the trick he had used in the past with showing the K-bar and yanking hands apart, Holiday took a TA-1 hand crank phone. Placing the two leads on the man's scrotum, he cranked the phone. This sent electrical shocks to the man's body. No damage, but it hurt like hell. Sgt. Jacobson glared at Holiday. "You taking Flower's place now"? Holidays realized Sarge was correct. He had judged Flowers and here he was, torturing the enemy. He threw the phone onto a rack, and walked out, muttering, "I have been here too long".

Days later, Holiday learned that the baby had been killed with that punch. Nothing was done to the marine. This was war. This was not murder. It was an attempt to stop a baby from crying and giving away the position, with the knowledge that 200 VC were advancing and no one knew how close. No one will understand. No one could, unless they had experienced what all these men who saw death almost daily saw.

> 24 Dec:67 Christmas Eve. The Captain had ordered 150 cases of San Miguel beer, in lieu of getting 160 cases of C rations. I do not know how he did it. I guess with some wheeling and dealing. But this is to be our Christmas present from the Captain. The grunts are getting about a case for each man. That's a hell of a lot of beer. San Miguel is a Filipino beer. It tastes like tiger piss.

"Hey, come get your beer". *My what?* Holiday pushed back the poncho that acted as a door to his hooch. He had been on an all-night patrol...again. Holiday saw marines running to the LZ, where cases of beer were being unloaded. Given that some were nondrinkers, it evened out to about a case per marine. The captain was there telling the marines, only those NOT on watch were allowed to drink. Those that got off watch could drink themselves silly after wards.

This was a VERY unusual event. Apparently the captain was missing "home for the Holidays" and knowing most felt the same way, ordered the beer as his Christmas present for the men. Holiday was not much of a drinker and wound up selling most of his for a buck a can.

Later on that night, the gun crews got a few poker games going, one in each gun crew hooch and one in the FDC hooch. Holiday was not used to being on the hill at night, since he spent most nights setting up ambushes. Not being able to sleep, Holiday got up from his cot and stumbled over to the FDC hooch. Everyone was talking about home and family, Christmases past, gifts they had gotten, girlfriends and happier times. And everyone was slowly getting drunk. Holiday could not relate to the happier times, home and hearth bullshit, so he wandered up to the CP hooch.

He remembered the last thing his step-mother had said to him at the Philadelphia Airport, while his father went to check on military stand -by openings, for a flight to California, on his way to Vietnam. His step-mother had grabbed his arm and said "I hope they kill you, you son of a bitch. We will be rid of you, once and for all". *Yeah Yeah, missing home...*

The captain was already shit faced drunk. He heard gunny telling him, if we got hit tonight we would get over run, since everyone had been drinking. Captain, took this as a challenge, grabbed a flare gun, inserted a flare and with drunken bravado, yelled at someone to point his arm to the sky. He had been swinging the flare gun all around, trying to find the night sky. Gunny finally grabbed his arm and forced it skyward. The skipper shot off the round. A red flare meant imminent attack and everyone was to go to their holes and other assigned areas and prepare to take on the enemy.

Holiday stood back as he watched drunken marines

scrambling all over the hill, grabbing flak jackets and helmets, rifles and ammo. Holiday jogged back to the nearest gun pit and started opening up boxes of mortars while the gun crew set up the gun.

The hill erupted into a roar as every weapon in their arsenal began shooting, including the mortars and grenades. Through the din, an order was given to cease fire, but the marines were too drunk to listen and kept firing. Being drunk, they were having too much fun. Finally one could hear over the din, "Don't shoot. Don't shoot. Snoopy is lost. Don't shoot Snoopy". Snoopy was a dingo that had become the company mascot. He had been taught to stalk and ambush. But the noise had frightened him so badly that he had run off into the night.

One hundred and sixty Marines began calling for Snoopy. "Snoopy, Snoopy, here Snoopy." Holiday found it quite amusing. All these Marines, just seconds earlier had put out thousands of rounds, shot several mortars and threw even more grenades, in their attempt to kill whomever was there that prompted the red flare. But with the mascot lost, they all softened their heart, to cease attempting to kill, now, to search for an animal.

Finally someone called out. "We found him" and a tremendous cheer went up from the entire company. Snoopy had got himself caught in the concertina, rolled barbed wire. It probably saved his life and was a miracle that he did not get shot. The marines drifted off to their poker games and memories of home and the night became silent. A silent night, but not a holy night.

The next morning, the villagers told the marines that there had been 800 VC waiting at the bottom of the hill. According to the villagers, they had been scheduled to attack at 0100, but the output of firepower that 160 drunk marines had sent down the hill, from a drunken order by the Captain to show the gunny there were still capable of fighting, had discouraged the VC from actually initiating the attack. The skipper had shot his red flare at 20 minutes to one. Perhaps it had been a Holy night after all. No one had died.

> 11Jan:68 Saw a marine get shot in the head today and live. Made a promise to myself. I am changing careers. This one is too damn dangerous.

It was one of those dark wet days. The clouds hung low and very dark. The patrol was sloshing through a rice paddy when a machine gun opened up on them. Marines scattered everywhere, but all made it to the relative safety of the dikes.

Now came the snipers. It was as if the machine gun was going to try for a mass kill, but now with everyone lying down behind rice paddy dikes, the snipers would attempt to pick them off, one by one.

When the machine gun had opened up, Holiday had

been on top of one dike with most marines ahead of him in the paddy. He had jumped down, actually slipped down the edge of the dike hitting the base of his spine hard. It hurt like hell. But like all the other marines, he stayed put wondering how in hell they would get out of this one.

Usually they would try to advance when caught in open ground but the machine gun and the fact that running through full paddies slows down how fast one can go, deterred any advancement, since it made the grunts much easier targets for a machine gun. The lieutenant kept hollering at everyone not to move. The grunts were so wet that their uniforms blended perfectly with the vegetation. Any movement would give the snipers an easy target.

One marine, lying to the right side of Holiday was trying to adjust his ammo belt to get easier access to his ammo when a sniper shot him in the helmet. Holiday saw his head snap back and the marine fall backwards into the water. He was certain the marine was dead. The corpsman was yelling at him to get the man's head out of the water before he drowns. Drowns? Hell, the man is dead, but Holiday did what he was told and crawled over to the marine, pulled his face out of the water, then leaned back against the edge of the dike waiting for the doc to get to him.

The snipers took a few shots at doc, but missed. Doc,

out of breath, grabs the helmet and yanks it off the grunt's head. Holiday fully expected to see a helmet full of brain, but what he did see was a big goose egg on the left side of the man's forehead.

The bullet had hit the helmet at an angle, spun completely around the helmet between the helmet and liner, destroying the liner and exiting the entry hole. It had knocked the grunt out and given him a nice goose egg.

Doc pulled out a razor and cut the man right on the goose egg. "What the hell are you doing, Doc?" Holiday inquired. The corpsman looks up. "No blood, no purple heart and this man deserves a purple heart". Doc started slapping the unconscious man to wake him up. With a groan and a cuss, the injured marine says, groggily, "What the fuck happened?

Doc yells at him. "You got shot in the head." This marine here wanted to give you mouth to mouth but I had to stop him. I think he is queer" "Fuck you, doc," Holiday muttered.

Doc explained what had happened and ended by saying, "You are a lucky man; and if this marine had not pulled your head out of the water, you might have drowned". Just *like doc, to not take the credit,* thought Holiday.

They stayed pinned down for another 3 hours, with the sniper taking pot shots at anything that moved. Three hours is a long time to sit in a cold wet rice paddy, and think. Holiday thought to himself, *"I am so sick of death and dying". If I ever get out of here alive I want to do something life enhancing, something positive and constructive, something like teach" "Yeah, to become a teacher, would be rewarding and positive and everyone needs an education if they want to improve their lives".* So, Holiday vowed to himself that he would go onto college, using the GI bill and become a teacher.

Finally, it got dark enough for the patrol to move out. The lieutenant decided that before the sniper brought his friends down under the cover of darkness, his patrol would be halfway back to their hill.

> 16 Jan :68 Sgt Mueller had taken me out of the bush. I was now a shortimer, and he felt I had done my time in the bush. He was using me as FDC radioman, while Horner, his replacement, had taken over as FO radioman. But Horner went and got himself shot. The radio on his back had saved his life. A patrol was withdrawing from the other side of the river under fire, when the bullet tore into his radio and lodged in his upper back. The river was still swollen from the monsoon rains and he ditched the radio while a fellow marines dragged his ass back across to our side of the river. So, guess who the FO radioman is again. That shitbird, Hawks had been shit-canned to Battalion HQ, where he could do the least amount of damage.

Six weeks left and Holiday was back on night patrols and ambushes. He had hated the lack of action on the hill. Shit duties, quick runs into Battalion HQ for pogie bait and smokes for the guys, anything to keep him from thinking too much about what he had already experienced.

He had grown sullen and distant, staying to himself. He remembered the night the village was attacked and the VC had kept the Marines on the hill by shooting as much at them as they did the PFs in the vil. The gun crews were throwing out HE rounds as fast as they could be unpacked, prepped and dropped down the tube.

Holiday had humped several cases of rounds from the ammo pit and was now busy tearing off increments and slipping off the safety pin then handing them to the "A" gunner. Each round had up to 9 increments attached near the fins. Distance depended as much on the number of increments as the elevation of the mortar gun. That night, all but 2 increments were taken off per each round.

Holiday could see tracer rounds zipping all around the hill from VC fire. But he was thinking more about saving the increments for more rat shooting contests. Every marine would catch live or dead rats. The increments were packed into the cylindrical mortar container then the live or dead rats were dropped in and a lit increment dropped down the tube. With a POOF the now charred rat would sail through the air at crude targets. The games were judged on accuracy and distance, with each gun team pitted against the other. Great fun.

Smiling to himself, Holiday noticed that Smoltz, the gunner was now standing upright dropping rounds down the tube and the tracer rounds were just inches over his head.

"Hey Smoltz" Holiday called out. "Those tracers are right over your head. I'd get down on one knee if I were you." Holiday had said it so calmly that Smoltz, dropping down to a knee, started screaming "Why the hell didn't you tell me?" "I just did" Holiday smiled.

Even in the darkness Holiday could catch the look from the other marines. It was one of disgust and contempt, that he had been so casual about telling Smoltz. *"Well,"* thought Holiday, *"they are not used to getting shot at so I guess they are near panic".*

Holiday then realized the real reason Mueller had pulled him out of the bush. Not to save him from possible death, since he was a short timer, but to give him time to adjust to NOT having to fight and kill. Death had become too casual a thing. Danger was too routine. It is then that combat marines begin making mistakes that endanger not only themselves, but those around them. Holiday had treated the danger to Smoltz as an " Oh, by the way, you might die"...way too casually.

2 Feb:68 Tet. A truce had been called but no one on the hill had been told. The grunts were still doing day and night patrols and I am still going out on them twice a day. Its better than burning shitters. We were orderd off the hill and the entire company found itself flown to hill

189

37 , Battalion HQ, the French fort just above the hamlet of Dai Loc. Seems attacks from the VC were being done all over the country. From the Delta near Saigon to the city of Hue the old capital city, near the DMZ.

"Hey Holiday, get your ass up and start packing. We're leaving". *What the hell?*

Holiday threw back the poncho to his hutch, rubbed his eyes and queried, "What do you mean; we are leaving...another patrol? I just got off one a couple of hours ago"

"Pack" came back the reply. "We are leaving the hill"

Holiday jogged up to the FDC hooch. He saw a flurry of activity all over the hill. Ammo was being hauled up to the LZ, gear of all sorts as well. "Hey Sarge, what's this all about" he asked Sgt Mueller. "Holiday", Mueller ordered," Help the guys destroy everything we can't take with us, then report to CP: the skipper wants to see you."

Holiday did as ordered. Holiday heard "fire in the hole" a lot that day, as Marines set up claymores and grenades and C4 to blow up all the hooches. Holiday watched a Marine deliberately walk into one of the gun pits as "fire in the hole" was being called. As the explosion ripped apart the ammo dump that was part of the gun pit, he watched the Marine grab his lower leg and go down. *That was deliberate* thought Holiday. He was setting himself up to get a million dollar wound. (a wound that would take him out of action but have no lasting or crippling damage).

Holiday was torn between feeling disgust for this act of cowardice and feeling empathy. Holiday had been in enough firefights, seen enough damage done to young bodies by booby-traps and snipers, heard enough cries of pain, and anguish, felt enough fear, his own and that of other marines, to understand why this grunt did what he did. Holiday turned his back and walked up to the CP.

"Lance Corporal Holiday reporting as ordered, sir." "Holiday, you are going to be my radioman for the day. "Stow your gear at the LZ and report back to me" "Aye aye , sir" Holiday had no gear to stow. All he had was a poncho, his radio, .45, and a carton of smokes. Holiday took the opportunity to head off the hill and give his carton of Marlboros to Grannysan, the old woman whose garden he had trashed accidentally when Lima Company had first occupied Hill 52, whom had befriended him and cooked up the dog meat dinner for him.

He saw Grannysan leaning on her hoe, taking a rest from tending to her garden. Approaching her, he offered his carton of smokes with both hands which is the traditional act of respect to her. This feisty woman, who had chewed him out when he had first stumbled through her garden 9 months ago, dropped her hoe and embraced him, crying into his chest. At that moment, Holiday felt the tenderest feeling he had experienced since landing in Da Nang on 5 February, 1967.

He was going to miss these people, Grannysan, the kids, the old man he used to play slappsies with, even the barber. They were just farmers, peasants, trying to live a normal life in a war torn county; a war they did not want nor understand. After the initial fear and suspicion had subsided in the early days, the villagers had befriended the Marines as much as the Marines had befriended them. Babies had been killed. One baby, a toddler had picked up an errant m79 round to play with. Somehow it had gone off and killed her. Young men and fathers had been murdered by the VC as Marines slept. Yet through it all a bond had been created between simple village people and powerful well-armed fighting men from a different culture.

By now it was late afternoon. Holiday made it back to the CP which was situated next to the LZ which could accommodate only one chopper at a time. CH-46's had begun flying in to take equipment and gear off the hill. Holiday took up his post of monitoring all radio traffic and informing the Skipper of any developments.

It was getting dusk and off in the distance Holiday could see hundreds of NVA making their way towards his hill. NVA! Not VC. Holiday started to get nervous as the sky darkened and he realized there were only a few Marines left on the hill. A radio call interrupted the darkness. A pilot called in asking if there were any friendlies off the hill.

"Sir, the pilot wants to know if we have any friendlies off the hill" "Hell no" came the reply from the Captain. Holiday repeated what the skipper had told him to the pilot. He could not hear any fighter jets or even gunships in the sky and wondered who the hell had asked about friendlies.

In the darkness Holiday could see what seemed like a solid stream of tracer rounds piercing the night sky, just south of the hill. Puff! It was Puff the Magic Dragon shooting his 6 barreled mini-gun, rate of fire was 100 rounds a second or 6000 rounds a minute.

Puff was a converted C-47 a vintage, post WWII cargo plane.

Holiday was mesmerized by the site of those tracer rounds, when he heard the skipper order him on the last ch-46 chopper leaving the hill. Just in time too. There were tracer rounds flying towards the hill from the East, North and South. The chopper did not waste any time. As soon as the Captain stepped aboard, the chopper lifted off and made a bee line towards Battalion on Hill 37.

7Feb: 68 Half the company stayed on Hill 37 while the other half went to Hill 65 about a quarter mile away. They put me on night guard duty for the 5 days I was there. I was used to being up all night, so no big deal. No attacks on Hill 37 or Hill 65, but Hill 41 was attacked and Hill 10 was over run again. Kilo Company held Hill 41. I was ordered to Hill 65 along with one gun crew.

The Company was going back to retake the hill. Holiday was ordered not to go. Sgt Mueller told him he was too short. (Shortimer, one who is leaving soon) "But, Sarge" Holiday pleaded, "Who do you have to be FO Radioman?" Holiday wanted badly to reclaim the hill. It had been his home for the past 9 months and it bothered him that they had given up the hill without a fight. Never mind that the reports said there were 2000 NVA soldiers bearing down on a hill with only 160 Marines on it.. NVA soldiers were tough and they stood and fought, unlike the hit and run VC. But, Holiday reasoned, they had taken on a regiment of NVA on Operation Arizona and beat them back......

"We'll be taking India Company's FO team," answered Miller. "You'll be doing security here on Hill 65, until your orders are cut and you didi out of here" (didi-Vietnamese slang for leave). Sgt Mueller extended his hand, "We will retake our hill and we won't be coming back, so this is goodbye. You have been a good FO and radioman and a good Marine". Holiday shook Mueller's hand. "Thanks, Sarge".

It took the company 5 days to retake Hill 52. The

reports said that they had to fight the whole way back. The story coming back, that when the Marine's finally stood on Hill 52 once again, the villagers had told them that before the last helicopter was out of site , the one Holiday was on, the NVA had raised their flag up the hill's flagpole.

Holiday spent those days, and the next 15 standing watch at night and sneaking over to hill 37, less than a mile away and hanging out in the Battalion radio shack, during the day, to get all the news of what was happening in the bush.

From what Holiday could gather, there were fire fights and battles all over the region. The fact was that the Marines had not lost any battle throughout the entire Tet offensive. He heard reports on Khe Sanh and Hue, to the North of Dai Loc. Holiday was grateful he was not in on any of these battles. He was content to hang around on Hills 65 and 37 waiting for orders to leave Nam.

Holiday would climb up on the wall of the French fort, on Hill 37 and spend his time thinking. From his vantage point, he could see the bridge the CBs had built and reflect back to the time some kids had sold the bridge security pot and remember that the VC had just strolled up to the bridge at dusk one day and blew away the Marines guarding the bridge. The Marines on the other side of the bridge said they had witnessed the other Marines waving and saying hello to the VC as they approached the bridge.

Holiday could almost see Hill 10 and remember the night, they got over run and Holiday had shot that VC coming at him wanting to bayonet him. He remembered being on Hill 41, further up the road from Hill 10, and going on those night ambushes with that 90 day wonder Lieutenant, who had ordered him not to go out with 2 canteens of water.

Those 15 days Holiday waited for orders were the worst 15 days of the entire tour. With nothing to do but stand watch at night, Holiday had the time to remember: Charlie dying to save him, killing those 2 VC with nothing but his 2 hands, watching Ramos die, watching that man holding his guts in his hands and crying for his mama, watching Henderson's head snap back in that mortar attack, carrying that marine to the chopper who had lost his leg , getting trapped in that irrigation ditch and watching doc flip off the VC, putting his finger into a wound to plug a chest wound....so many memories.

Why did he survive when better men did not? Was it just fate, or did God have a hand in who lived and who died? IF... that bullet had been a couple of inches lower, it would have gone through his helmet and through his brain, instead of popping his camouflage cover. IF...that bullet had been one inch closer to the right, it would have gone through his eye and into his brain instead of chipping stone off the building he was hiding behind.

IF...he had failed to turn in time to see that bayonet coming at his gut, he would have been skewered and killed, that same night Ramos was killed. IF... that shrapnel that snapped his antenna off his radio had been a little closer, it would have gone into his face. IF... Charlie had ducked instead of jumping in front of him, he would be alive and Holiday would be dead. IF........If IF was a horse we'd all take a ride. Was it fate? Or was there purpose too all of this?

In the twelve months and twenty-two days he had been in this country, he had seen the cruelest acts that mankind can do to itself and had also seen the noblest acts of love and courage that any man can do. Did not the Bible say "Greater love hath no man than to lay down his life for his brother"? Was this all part of a grand design? Was there purpose in Charlie's sacrifice? Was there purpose in Holiday's life? What does it all mean?

What Holiday did know was that he had seen and done too much. He would have to live with his memories and he would have to learn from his experiences. Would he be able to teach others what he had learned? Some day he may have children. What kind of father would he be? The same hands that squeezed the life out of his enemy would be the same hands that would hold his baby with love.

Holiday withdrew within himself. He did not socialize with the other Marines. He did not want to hear about men missing their girlfriends back in the world, or missing family, or hearing stories from the funewgies coming over. He did not care to know what the latest songs were how styles had changed, where other Marines were from. He did not want to hear about "home". He had no home to go to. He decided once he got out of the corps he would use his GI bill and keep his promise to himself, when he was pinned down in that rice paddy, to get a degree and become a teacher. Perhaps, then, as he helped shape young minds in a free society, all of this would have been worth it.

GLOSSARY

SEATO: South East Asia Treaty Organization

MOS: military occupational specialty

FO: forward observer (in the field)

FDC fire directional control (in the rear)

NCOIC: noncommissioned officer in charge (enlisted person usually sergeant or higher)

LAW: Light Anti-tank Weapon; a one shot then throw away improvement of the old WW II 3.5 rocket launcher, commonly known as a bazooka

KIA: Killed In Action

vil: short for village

PRC 25: Portable Radio Combat: A portable radio weighing about 30 pounds, carried on the back

Gung-ho: a hard charger, very dedicated and devoted to the Marine Corps

Half-step: not giving 100% effort

WIA: Wounded In Action

Hooch: take on "hutch", to describe any flimsy structure, such as a Vietnamese house made of bamboo, or a living quarter for Marines made of sandbags.

ARVN: Army of the Republic of Viet Nam

Water Bo: water buffalo

OP : Observation Post. Usually 2-4 men sent out beyond the perimeter to watch for any movement that might threaten the main body of Marines

CP: Command Post. On patrol, depending on the size of the patrol, the CP was the Lieutenant, or Captain if it was company size along with his radioman, his exec (a lieutenant) or staff NCO , such as a gunnery sergeant or a staff sergeant and the support group, the FO and radioman, a corpsman, interpreter if one is available

fire team: a unit of 4 men and a part of a squad which consists of 2 or 3 fire teams.

Squad: part of a platoon, which consists of usually 3 or 4 squads

Platoon: part of a company which consists of usually 3 platoons

Company: part of a battalion which in the Marine Corps consists of 4 companies.

Battalion: part of a regiment which in the Marine Corps consists of 3 battalions

fire fight: battle

H E: High Explosive In radio language, called Hotel Echo, to identify the type of 81 mortar to be used.

Willy Peter aka Whiskey Papa: to identify a white phosphorous round, used to mark a location.

Fire mission: using the radio to call in a mortar attack. The fire mission usually consisted of one willy peter to mark a location then fire was adjusted from that point, usually with another white phosphorous round, but sometimes the initial location was so close that the next order was to fire 10 rounds HE (hotel echo) and fire for effect, i.e. blast the hell out of that location.

RADIO CALL SIGNS

Crepe Myrtle: battalion HQ

Whiskey: 81 mortars

Lima: Lima Company

Lima 1: First platoon

Lima 1 Actual: first platoon lieutenant

Crepe Myrtle Whiskey: 81 headquarters at battalion

Whiskey Lima: 81 mortars attached to Lima Co

Whiskey Lima Forward: the 81 mortar team in the field

Lima 6: the company commander usually a Captain

Lima 1/3 first platoon 3rd. squad

Skipper: the Captain or company commander

Top: Top sergeant for the company Usually E-8 or above

Gunny: Gunnery Sergeant E-7

ENLISTED RANKS

E: enlisted pay grade

E1 private

E2 private first class (Pfc)

E3 Lance Corporal

E4 Corporal

E5 Sergeant's

E6 Staff Sergeant's

E7 Gunnery Sergeant

E8 Master Sergeant or First Sergeant

E9 Master Gunnery Sergeant or Sergeant Major

snuffy: a low ranking person equivalent to a serf or servant

Funewgy (fun ew' gy): a Fucking NEW GuY

"Mickey Mouse": To focus on the trivial or cartoonish aspects of being a Marine. For example, berating a Marine for having a button unbuttoned after wading through a leach-infested pond.

M-79: a breech loading grenade launcher that shot one 79 mm

round at a time. It looked like an oversized, short barreled shotgun.

LP: a listening post, usually of 2 men, placed on the outside of a defensive perimeter to watch and listen for enemy movement.

Gook: a derogatory term aimed at VC or VC sympathizers

S.O.P. Standard Operating Procedure

CIDG: Vietnam's version of a militia

RPG: Rocket Propelled Grenade

Amtrak: Amphibious Tracked vehicle, shaped like a shoe box; used to transport troops or supplies on land or in water.

POWs Prisoner of war

<u>Bald Eagle: A company sized unit sent to rescue another unit</u>

Sparrow hawk: A platoon sized unit sent to rescue another unit